THE CHALLENGE OF SHORE ANGLING

THE CHALLENGE
OF
SHORE ANGLING

A PRACTICAL GUIDE

Lindsey Green

WARD LOCK

First published in Great Britain in 1991
by Ward Lock, Villiers House, 41/47 Strand, London WC2N 5JE

British Library Cataloguing in Publication Data
Green, Lindsey
    First steps in shore angling.
    1. Coastal waters. Shore angling
    I. Title
    799.16

ISBN 0706 3 6945 9

Printed and bound in Great Britain by Courier International

To my wife, Julie Green,
and in memory of my father, Captain Cyril Green,
from whom I inherited a love of the sea.

Acknowledgements

I would like to thank the following for their photographic contributions to this book: Martin Edge of Hamworthy in Poole for the underwater shots; Terry Lamburn and Mike Bailey of The Sportsman, Paignton; Phil Hyde of South West Tackle in Paignton.

Front jacket picture, back jacket picture, pp. 1, 2, 3 (top) 4, 5 colour section, courtesy of Russell Symons. Colour Section p. 7 courtesy of John Watson.

I would also like to thank Guy Milham, Editor of *Sea Fishing* magazine, for his support and advice over the years.

Contents

What's out there? Big wrasse perhaps. Feeding actively in the warm water, coming in on the tide over the rocks, hunting for sea slaters or shrimps; or maybe pollack, if the rocks beneath the surface provide weed cover from which to launch an ambush

CHAPTER ONE

The Right Approach

At the age of 17 I began to research thoroughly all types of fishing, analyzing techniques to discover ways of improving my catch rate. Since then I have successfully used carp and river tactics for shore angling, experimented with fly tackle and produced several of my own tackle designs.

In this book I have collected together all of the best methods that I tried and still use today, from basics to tackles designed for a specific purpose. Chapter by chapter I hope to lead the newcomer to a point where he feels confident of being able to fish effectively from the shore. For the more experienced anglers I have tried to demonstrate some new ideas and show them ways of saving money on tackle.

To start with I am going to introduce some general ideas on both fish and the sea itself. If you look at the photograph on page 10 you will see some pout grubbing about for food. Notice especially the one at the bottom of the picture, who seems to be rubbing his head on the rocks. What he is doing is using both scent and taste to help him find something to eat.

Fish senses

You can also see that the other fish have a barbel on their lower jaw. This is studded with extra taste cells to help them find food as they root around on the bottom, compensating slightly for the lessening of sight as the shoal moves into deeper water. Despite the comparatively large eyes and the swivel action that allows fish a greater field of vision, their dependence on sight is not as great as it is for a human. The water in which they live acts as a filter, draining both light and colour to the point where the fish

must depend on additional senses. This assistance takes the form of an in-built sonar that enables them to find their path in much the same way as a bat does in the air.

In the second photograph a prowling cod is highlighted in the glare of a diver's lamp. Along its flanks there is a line clearly delineated in white. This is called the lateral line. As the fish swims, the vibrations of its movement are transmitted through the water. Consequently its presence may be detected through the lateral lines of other fish, warning them of its approach. At the same time these vibrations are deflected by objects in the path of the fish, bouncing back to be detected by the cod's lateral line and enabling it to steer a course without bumping into anything.

For hunting, this additional sense is invaluable, but it leads to the evolution in the different species of tactics that are essential for survival. The humble blenny (see p. 3 of colour plates) hides in a small hole in the rocks from which it pounces on scraps and darts back to its lair, hugging the rocks all the while so that the background echo confuses any predator. Larger fish, like the pollack, develop new ways of hunting. This species has evolved a protruding lower jaw. It hides in ambush and attacks prey from below, where its extended jaw enables it to seize its target more efficiently.

Locating fish

In each chapter I will deal with likely places to catch fish and ways of turning each species' habits to your own advantage. For now it will pay to consider your quarry in terms of vibration, scent and taste. If you can develop tackles that enhance your bait's

Pouting grubbing for food

natural attraction you are thinking on the right lines. Bear in mind also your choice of location. If there are swimmers in the water then beach fishing is out. Similarly, with rocky locations, if there are crab pots in the area then they will be continually laying up a scent trail around where you are fishing.

Don't just go to the shore and throw out a line. Use the shape of the environment itself to help you choose where to fish. Keep notes on the spots that you visit and build up a picture based on your own experience. Note what the weather was like, whether there were spring or neap tides, at what state of the tide you fished and, just as important, what was the response to the methods you tried.

Take float-fishing for mackerel. How deep were you fishing? Remember that warm water is lighter than cold, so that on a particularly warm day the fish may move nearer to the surface than is their usual custom. Similarly, on a cold day they may go deeper. Where there is a power station then the chances are that the outfall of warm water will attract fish in droves, heating up the local environment and perhaps even persuading predators such as bass to stay in the area for longer than usual.

As for the tides, they affect fishing in several ways. The sea is influenced by the gravitational pull of both the sun and the moon. During a spring tide

Cod in the glare of the diver's lamp

the gravitational pull of each of these bodies acts in unison. Consequently a greater amount of water is affected, which builds up as the earth rotates and then swells against the land. It recedes and begins the process again for the next high tide.

During a neap period the gravitational pull of the sun and moon are working against each other. Less water is affected and the tides are noticeably lower at high water and higher at low water. Thus during spring tides high water is considerably higher and much more beach is exposed at the low tide. Consequently it is easier to obtain bait during a spring period than a neap.

With experience you will find that most spots fish better at certain states of the tide. An example is Hope's Nose in Torbay. During August most fishing is at its best at the top two hours of the high tide, with mackerel, garfish, pollack and mullet coming regularly to the net. Bass show very well when these hours fall during the early part of the morning. However, at the bottom two hours of the low tide there are spots where you can be reasonably sure of flatfish and gurnard, with the occasional black bream making an appearance. The trick is to pick a likely spot and stay with it until it becomes familiar.

Pay particular attention to both estuaries and headlands. When an estuary is created it acts as a

Catch of wrasse

tunnel into which the sea pours with great force. On the other hand, a headland disrupts the pattern, causing the formation of fierce currents that sweep around its end. If you plan to fish during a rising tide at either locality you will probably need to increase the size of your weight to counter the strong flow that will be met. At such places it is best to use spiked leads, which grip the seabed better.

Handling fish
When you eventually catch fish you must be careful how you handle them, for their bodies are covered with a thin epidermis that protects them

against infection. If you intend to return a fish to the water, be sure to handle it with a wet rag to prevent damage.

It may also be advisable — though this is a matter for the individual — to purchase a keepnet. This is a long, hooped net with soft mesh more often used by coarse anglers. Once laid out in the water, fish can swim up and down in it in reasonable comfort. In this way the angler can keep the fish alive and select those that he wishes to retain at the end of the day, returning the rest of the catch to the water.

If you look at the photograph you will see a catch of wrasse that I kept for a while and then returned.

They all shot off without injury and, had I been fishing in a competition, the keepnet would have allowed me to select the biggest for weighing in.

Angling clubs

It may be beneficial to join an angling club. Most are only too pleased to welcome newcomers and it can be pleasant to have someone helping you to progress and generally taking an interest. Usually a club represents a considerable pool of both experience and expertise, extremely useful for anyone just starting. However, if you are a family man then find out what the club has to offer youngsters. Some clubs are happy to welcome them, while a few cannot be bothered.

Whether you join a club or not, it pays to buy the NFSA (National Federation of Sea Anglers) diary. This contains information on the tides and a list of minimum sizes below which fish should be returned alive to the water. This practice is intended to ensure that fish get at least one chance to breed before being killed and eaten. Some of the sizes are a bit small but later on I will give a more precise indication of the size at which certain species attain sexual maturity.

CHAPTER TWO

Choosing Tackle

I would advise anyone wanting to start fishing to go on a few trips with friends who already fish. This will give them a taste of the sport without laying out money on tackle. If they decide that it really is not what they want, at least they will not be out of pocket.

It is not cheap to start fishing, but in this chapter I will go through the essential equipment and try to pick out some of the best choices from the wide range available. I am not about to produce a comprehensive tackle guide — my aim is simply to get you started. The frills can come later.

If you have not got a rod, or indeed any major piece of tackle, bear in mind that prices vary considerably. If you go to a local tackle shop you may well find that you quickly establish a rapport with the owner. Most owners will readily advise you about tackle and are a good source of information on which spots are fishing well. But be prepared to pay the maximum retail price in small shops, as they have to purchase their stock through wholesalers.

An alternative is the major retailers who advertise in the angling press. Many offer substantial discounts on rods and reels, even giving interest-free credit for several months. As there is competition between the mail-order shops, it usually pays to ring around to compare prices and go for the cheapest.

RODS

Over the last few years considerable advances have been made in rod-building materials. What has emerged today is an upper bracket of high-performance casting tools made out of carbon-fibre, semi-carbon, whisker-kevlar and boron, with the ingredients mixed in differing percentages. At the lower end of the range there is a wide choice of fibre-glass rods offering both reliability and sufficient casting power for the majority of fishing situations. Many are perfectly good but be cautious about the very cheapest, as these are often clumsy and lack the capacity for distance casting.

Fibre-glass lacks several of the advantages of carbon-fibre and the more sophisticated materials. It is heavy by comparison and not as stiff as the newer developments. A fibre-glass butt (the section that includes the handle) often fails to produce the inflexibility required at this point and gives under pressure, drawing power away from the tip of the rod, where it is needed. This does not happen as often with carbon-fibre, which is very stiff and resistant to such pressure, although it is more easily damaged by lateral stress — if you step on it, for example.

Leaving aside the difference in performance, fibre-glass does have the advantage of price. Carbon-fibre and most of the composites are still very expensive, although there is increasingly available a wide range of budget-priced semi-carbons. In some cases these are quite reasonable in price, particularly carp rods for use with spinning and float tackle. But as for beachcasters, the superlative examples will continue to make a sizeable hole in your pocket for some time to come.

Beachcasting rods

When you come to look at beachcasters you will probably hear a lot of people talking about tournament rods. These long-distance, high-performance blanks have been developed for casting competitions, where the aim is to send a 5¼ oz (150 gm) weight as far as possible with reasonable accuracy. These contests can be great fun, particularly when people such as Les Baldry, Neil McKellow and Paul Kerry are taking part, each of whom have cast over 260 yards (240 m). They make very enjoyable watching but such skill, particularly to newcomers, can be very daunting.

I've been on a tight budget for as long as I can remember, but I longed for one of those high-power rods with a yearning that was almost physical. At the time I had an old Woolworth beachcaster and a Garcia-Mitchell 602 AP multiplier. One day I decided to go to a local casting event and see what I could do. I was allowed six casts and, with a fourteen-year-old rod with nearly as old a reel, hit 146 yards (134 m) on each cast.

Other people cast a lot further than that but quite often they were one-offs, the average of their six casts falling below 146 yards (134 m). What I felt I had achieved was consistency. Later, when my wife gave me a fibre-glass Paul Kerry Supercast for my birthday, I increased my distance over grass to 180 yards (165 m). While that will never compete with the leading casters, nonetheless I was happy with it, particularly so because with that tackle and my style of casting I could feel that my bait would reach the fish appetizingly. Sometimes that doesn't happen with the top-of-the-range tournament rods, the bait being subjected to such stress that it can literally explode during a cast. And as for bite detection, some carbon rods are so stiff that the end barely twitches on a bite that would have set a fibre-glass rod rattling.

Long casting is a desirable goal and undoubtedly an advantage, but if you can consistently cast over 100 yards (90 m) you have nothing to be ashamed of. If that is your limit just make the best of it, making sure that you have good bait presentation and clear bite detection. Check on the spots that you intend to fish. One mark may fish well at distance, another better close in. Better yet, fish at night when some of the larger specimens occasionally rove into shallower water.

If you select your rod carefully a cast of over 100 yards (90 m) should not be difficult. Basing the specific measurements on beachcasting rods, I have listed below five points to help you choose.

1. Rings

The best rings are designed to reduce friction during a cast and minimize damage to the line by abrasion, particularly when winding in. You won't get the best out of cheap, poor-quality rings, so it is better to stick to the quality of, for example, the Daiwa Dynaflo range or the Fuji BSHGs.

You also need to consider both the number and size of rings to match not only the rod, but also the reel. If you want to use a fixed-spool reel the rings should be large. The diameter of the butt ring (nearest to the reel) should be about 50 mm, of the tip ring 16 mm and of the intermediates, from the top down, 20 mm, 25 mm, 30 mm and 40 mm. The reason for this is that a fixed-spool throws off loops of line during a cast. These rub around the rings but you can reduce this friction by siting them well up the rod. This gives the line a chance to straighten out a bit and, if the butt ring is situated 60 in (150 cm) away from the reel seat, the problem is minimized. As for the intermediates, working from the butt ring, the distance between them should decrease progressively until the smallest gap is to be found between the tip and the first ring. Measurements will depend on the length of the blank, but certainly the first should not be less than 6 in (15 cm) from the tip.

In the case of a rod intended for use with a multiplier, more and smaller rings should be used. The diameter of the butt ring might be 30 mm, spaced at least 40 in (100 cm) from the reel seat, while the tip ring could be between 12 mm and 16 mm. Intermediates might be 25 mm, 20 mm, 16 mm, 16 mm, 12 mm and 12 mm. Don't be tempted to use intermediates less than 10 mm as these are too small to cope with leader knots, casting and seaweed.

Whatever kind of rod you decide on, the rings must be in line and correctly spaced. A quick check is to put the rod together and look down the rings. What should be immediately evident is a neat, tunnel-like effect, the tip ring neatly framed by the first, the first by the second etc. If the rings are all over the place reject the rod.

2. The butt

This should be stiff enough not to fold under the pressure of a high-power cast. To test a rod in the shop, brace the bottom of the blank against the side of one foot and grab it with a hand about 5 ft (1.5 m) up the rod. Use the other hand to flex it, pushing roughly in the middle between your foot and hand. If it is sloppy don't buy it.

You will find on many beachcasters that the manufacturers have run the blank into an alloy tubing butt to overcome the problem of sloppy action. Another method used is to strengthen fibre-glass by reinforcing the lower section with carbon-fibre. Best of all is a pure carbon butt. With any rod, take a good look at the reel seat to make sure that it is strong and of good quality.

As for the position of the reel seat, this ultimately depends on your style of casting. Some pendulum casters have the reel seat at the bottom of the rod, slotting an additional piece of carbon tube into the blank for comfort when reeling in. Others prefer a more relaxed casting style with the reel seat 28–32 in (70–80 cm) from the bottom of the rod. This allows for comfortable positioning of the hands and is far easier for beginners to come to terms with.

A recent innovation is the replacement of the traditional reel seat with a pair of free-sliding coaster grips, allowing the angler complete flexibility as to where to position the reel. You simply put it in place, slide the grips over the feet and tighten them by rotating the knob. The grips then fasten on the blank in much the same way as a jubilee clip. No screwdriver or other tools are required.

Pay particular attention to the handle supplied with the rod. You will often need to hold it for long periods of time and so should choose something that you can grip in comfort. At one time cork was widely used but over the years the quality has deteriorated, opening up competition to the modern hypalon and moulded-rubber grips.

3. The tip

This should be slim, resilient and powerful, good for detecting bites and yet flexible enough to compress during the cast and immediately recover, hurling the weight seawards. Some fibre-glass blanks have thick, sloppy tips that compress during the cast but are slow to recover, failing to get power behind the weight. By contrast, some carbon rods have very stiff tips that fail to react in the way that you want.

A good compromise has been reached in the use of semi-carbons, with the result that you can get an excellent rod without the expense of pure carbon or sophisticated composites. Two companies well worth looking into are Zziplex and Conoflex, which offer a range of blanks that combine quality and power.

4. The spine

The way in which blanks are manufactured means that there is a plane that will bend a little more easily in a particular direction on every blank. Known as the spine or bias, this plane can be found by pressing on the rod as you slowly rotate it. The spine is important as it is the plane of maximum compression. Consequently all rings should be positioned exactly along it. If they are on the inside of the curve a slightly smoother cast can be obtained, whereas placing them on its outside leads to a perfectly straight rod.

Ignoring the spine is detrimental to the rod. Gradually it will acquire a harsh and unwieldy feel that is accented by high-power casting. In time you may even find that the whippings securing the rings work loose and cause them to fly off in use, perhaps even damaging the blank.

5. Joints

Where a blank is in two or more sections the joints should be well protected. Often these joints, or spigots, take the form of a thinner-diameter piece of glass tubing that fits tightly inside the tapering walls of the upper section. Consequently the exterior of the top section is subjected to a great deal of stress. This can fracture the walls of the blank if it is not strengthened by a good, tight whipping properly sealed with epoxy resin or varnish.

If you plan to build your own rod a good tip for the whippings is to treat them with cellulose dope, which shrinks the fibres and ensures good tension. You may find that some threads require treatment with a colour preserver before use, or they will go opaque. It is best to check this before purchase.

A fixed-spool reel with rear drag

There are several good-quality rod varnishes available which will seal the whippings after treatment, making them watertight, although an alternative is a clear epoxy resin. If you decide to use resin be careful when adding the hardener — too much and it sets too quickly, leading to flaws within the finish that will crack during casting and make the whippings look unsightly.

A last piece of advice to beginners is, if possible, to take an experienced angler with you when buying your first rod. His opinions will be based on experience and he is unlikely to be fooled by the many attractive but unsatisfactory models.

REELS

Two main types of reel are used by the sea angler — fixed-spool and the multiplier. The fixed-spool, as its name suggests, incorporates a spool fixed on the end of a spindle connecting to gears contained within a rear housing. A handle at the side of the reel rotates a line pick-up device (the bale arm) around the spool, distributing the line on the spool. With each turn of the handle the spindle rises and falls, ensuring that the line is evenly laid with regard to both height and depth. To make a cast the bale arm is manually disconnected and the line held by a finger until release, when line is stripped from the spool by the momentum of the cast. A turn of the handle after casting re-engages the bale arm.

The fixed-spool reel is difficult to tangle, unless overfilled, and retrieves line very quickly. Its main disadvantages are that it has a fairly insensitive 'drag' (the mechanism used to check the release of line when the bale arm is closed) which complicates the playing of fish, and that the line leaves the spool, during a cast, under steadily mounting resistance. This makes it difficult to empty, the resistance increasing with the distance from the rim of the spool to the body of line still on it.

For night fishing and use by the beginner, the fixed-spool is very suitable. It is also very efficient with light tackle such as a float rig. However, it can twist the line, which weakens it, particularly when the line is retrieved under minimal load or at high speed. The fixed-spool is a good first or light-tackle reel, but for beachcasting the multiplier is superior.

Some good fixed-spools are the DAM 5001, Shakespeare Sigma Gold 080, Shimano Biomasters nos GT7000 and GT8000, Sagarra Tarzan, Ryobi GX60, Mitchell 498 and 499 (left or right-hand wind) and the basic but efficient Daiwa DF90. All of these reels have been tried and tested and have excellent track-records.

The multiplier

The spool of the multiplier revolves with every turn of the handle. A flick of a switch disengages the gears and leaves the spool free-running for the release of line. This release is tempered by centrifugal braking systems, magnetic control or direct braking in which a metal plate presses against the spindle of the spool. Some form of braking is necessary to prevent the spool from running too fast during casting, otherwise it throws up great loops of line in a tangle — the infamous 'bird's nest'.

When retrieving the line, the gearing of a multiplier turns the spool several times for every turn of the handle, hence the name, multiplier. Its rate of retrieval is not as high as the fixed-spool's, however, so when you are fishing snaggy marks it cannot lift the terminal tackle off the bottom as quickly. This shortcoming can be partly remedied by filling the spool to its maximum capacity. Then, when you reel in, more line is retrieved because the surface diameter of the spool has been augmented with the additional line.

Some multipliers are fitted with a level-line device, which lays the line evenly upon the spool, performing a task usually done by the angler's thumb. Unfortunately this slows the reel during casting and decreases the length of the cast. Another disadvantage with some is that knots in the line can catch during casting and lead to bird's nests or even the loss of tackle, owing to the line snapping.

Centrifugal brakes employ either two or four brake blocks set to north, east, south and west of the central spindle on which the spool is mounted. These can be removed, but the braking power obviously lessens with each removal. It is usually best to keep two blocks until you are familiar with your reel, but as your confidence grows you can go down to one without much risk.

The multiplier is a finely tuned instrument that will react to any flaws in your casting style. Jerky casts frequently, if not invariably, lead to severe tangles, so the use of a multiplier calls for practice, as well as frequent lubrication and proper maintenance. In return they have silky-smooth drag systems, giving out line on demand to a running fish with far more sensitivity than a fixed-spool.

For lubrication of the gears, experiment with different grades of oil until you find the one that is best suited to your reel. It could be an SAE 10 or STP, or indeed any grade in-between.

The quality of the reel you choose depends on how much you spend, but a good inexpensive model is the rugged and dependable Mitchell 602AP. If you can afford a more sophisticated reel, choose from the ABU 6500 and 7000 series, Daiwa millionaires or Magforce PMF 57. Shimano multipliers such as the Triton TSM 2CFS are also well worth having a look at.

Further information on tuning and other adjustments that you might wish to make to your reel is given in the chapter on casting.

LINES

Three main types of line are available to the shore angler: nylon monofilament, wire (which may be plain, several strands twisted together, or even nylon-covered) and Dacron. By far the most popular is nylon, which varies widely in both price and performance.

A variety of cheaper lines are available in bulk spools, the basic criteria being that you get what you pay for. Drennan bulk spools offer a reasonable compromise between quality and cost, while TRILENE and MAXIMA are good quality lines at the higher end of the price range. ABU 'Fluo' lines are good quality, offering an excellent strength of line to diameter ratio, but personally I am very much put off by the fluorescent yellow coloration.

Whichever brand you decide upon, you will need line to fill your spool, line of a lower breaking strain for making traces (a short length of line between the hook and the leader) and some 50 lb (23 Kg) b.s. line for making leaders. A leader is a length of line three times the length of your rod which is tied to your main line and used to offset the stress inherent in casting. Some anglers use Dacron for leaders because its zero elasticity means that it does not draw power away from the cast, but this is a fine point and the benefit does not merit the additional expense.

Wire is used for making conger traces, so that the eels cannot bite their way to freedom and, in lesser breaking strains, is also used by some wrasse anglers for the same reason. For conger traces I use 45 lb (20 Kg) b.s. nylon-covered wire and for wrasse fishing would advise a breaking strain no greater than 20 lb (9 Kg).

Breaking strain

The breaking strain of the line that you choose will vary depending upon your geographical location and the type and size of fish that you expect to catch. For example, I do a lot of my fishing in Dorset and South Devon, where I use 12 lb (5.5 Kg) main line and 8 lb (3.5 Kg) trace. For rock fishing I use 18 lb (8 Kg) main line and unwaxed dental floss — which has a b.s. of about 12 lb (5.5 Kg) — for the traces. Dental floss is very supple, extremely difficult for fish to bite through and easy to colour.

Colouring of traces is a trick that is used to make the nylon — which glints underwater — become less noticeable and blend with its surroundings. The glint is reduced by marking the line with a broad-tipped permanent marker in any colour you like, although I prefer black, green or brown. Coloured green, dental floss acts like a thin strand of weed.

In some areas rock anglers will use 30 lb (14 Kg) main line, while beach anglers — who have to contend with floating masses of weed — may use main line of 20 lb (9 Kg) or 25 lb (11 Kg). It is wisest to seek advice from local anglers so that you can match your tackle to the requirements of your area.

WEIGHTS

It is not unusual to lose several weights during a session, particularly when fishing rocky marks. Consequently weights are a continuing expense, but one which can be much reduced by making your own. Fortunately for today's angler there are many varieties of moulds on the market, with excellent patterns available from Ajusti Moulds of Kingsteignton in Devon and also from DCA Moulds, both of which can be purchased either through shops or by mail order.

Several patterns of lead weights are available (Fig. 1) and quite often you hear people extolling the virtues of a particular type for casting. However, there is no significant difference between the aerodynamic performance of, say, a torpedo, an aquapedo, a beachbomb and an aquazoom. They are all efficient and it is simply a matter of personal choice. For example, I prefer aquapedos as they don't roll about in the tide quite as much as more rounded weights such as the beachbomb.

Making your own weights

Breakaways and cranstals are shop-bought leads, but all of the others mentioned above can be made at home. If you decide to make your own weights bear the following points in mind:

1. Molten lead gives off toxic fumes, so be sure that you work in an area with good ventilation.

2. Heat the mould before you pour any lead into it. This will save the weights from unsightly wrinkles and ensure that there is no moisture within the mould. Any damp is dangerous as contact with molten lead will cause a violent expulsion of steam under pressure.

3. Make sure that the mould is clamped tightly together before pouring. Besides the obvious vice or G-clamp you will find that a market-stall

FIG. 1 Lead weights

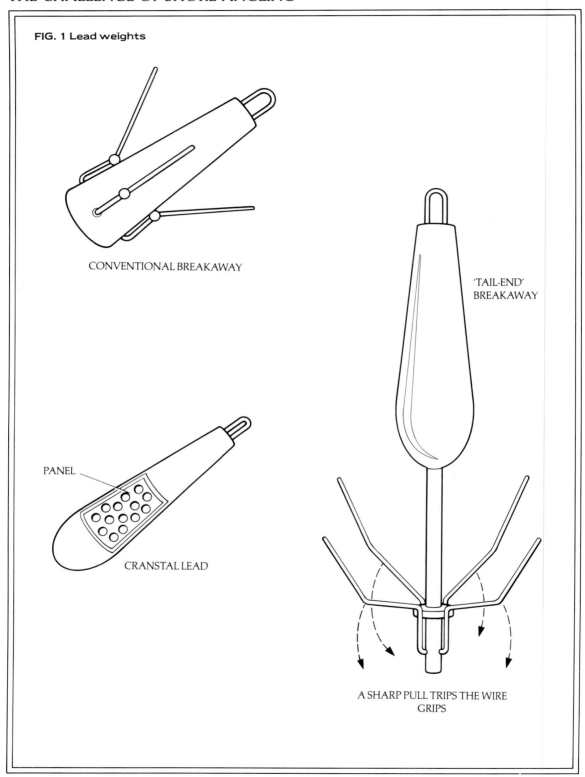

CONVENTIONAL BREAKAWAY

PANEL

CRANSTAL LEAD

'TAIL-END'
BREAKAWAY

A SHARP PULL TRIPS THE WIRE
GRIPS

clip does an excellent holding job and is very cheap.

4. Use a good-quality wire for the eye of the sinker. As it will take a lot of knocking about it needs to be strong — preferably in brass or stainless steel.

5. With spiked leads, the best place to site the wires is in the nose of the weight, not the sides. Generally, longer wires hold better to a sandy bottom, but this principle can be taken to extremes. Six inches (15 cm) of wire protruding from the nose and bent into a U-shape is often quite effective, but remember that you will need four such wires and that they should be well rooted in the body of the weight.

When you buy a mould it should come with instructions for use. These should advise the best method of securing wires for the model that you have purchased. It is also best to wear heat-resistant gloves, as after a single casting the mould will be so hot that it is dangerous to handle.

Drilled bullets — round weights that slide on the line — are useful in an assortment of sizes for both float-fishing and spinning. You will also need some spiked leads for fishing in strong tidal flows. Breakaway manufacture two quick-release models in which the spikes anchor the weight in the sand, but which can be tripped by a sharp pull so that the weight is freed and the wires trail behind the body of the sinker. Before recasting you simply reset the wires to their original position.

Of the two models, the long-tailed variety has greater holding power. For most situations the conventional 'breakaways' provide sufficient anchorage, but for really strong flows a 5 oz (150 gm) long-tail will provide roughly the same anchorage as a 7 oz (200 gm) conventional breakaway, enabling you to fish lighter.

Another commercial weight that attracts attention is the cranstal lead. This hollow sinker has a removable panel so that you can fill the body with cotton wool impregnated with a scent agent such as pilchard oil or Biotrak. Once the tackle settles on the bottom it lays a scent trail near your bait that attracts fish to it. Some people swear by it and quite a lot swear about it, but my own tests have proved inconclusive. (It's no longer produced).

SWIVELS AND LINKS

I am probably going to annoy some tackle manufacturers in this little section, but because so many of the swivels currently available are unnecessary I shall mention only one.

Swivels are used to prevent twisting of the line and sometimes to help change traces quickly. The most efficient swivel that I have ever tried is the Berkeley swivel, which I have never since been tempted away from. It is neat, strong and functional. If you want to change traces quickly simply add a stainless steel, oval split link to one eye of the swivel.

Split links are also useful for enabling you to change lead weights without dismantling the whole tackle. Do not be tempted to use cheaper wire alternatives. These are potentially very dangerous, as they might open during a cast and allow the weight to hurtle off, perhaps even killing someone. That may sound like fiction rather than fact, but people have been killed by lead weights.

A useful trick with Berkeleys is to adapt them for use with a type of tackle known as the paternoster (Fig. 2). Simply slide the swivel over a short length of plastic tubing and a piece of wire. Push it to the middle of the tube and secure it in position by coiling the wire to both sides of it as tightly as possible. If you support the plastic by sliding it over a nail or the smooth end of a drill bit, you can really pull the wire tight. This will make the finished job a lot neater.

HOOKS

These are the most important part of your tackle. No matter how much time and energy you devote to everything else, all your efforts will be wasted if you skimp on hooks.

Hooks come in a variety of patterns, sizes and makes, but although they all vary Fig. 3 identifies the common parts. The various shapes of eye have a bearing when you come to select the right hook for your bait. For example, an eyed hook will tear a worm as you thread it, whereas a ribbed shank, whipped and glued to the trace, will inflict far less

FIG. 2 Adapted Berkeley swivel

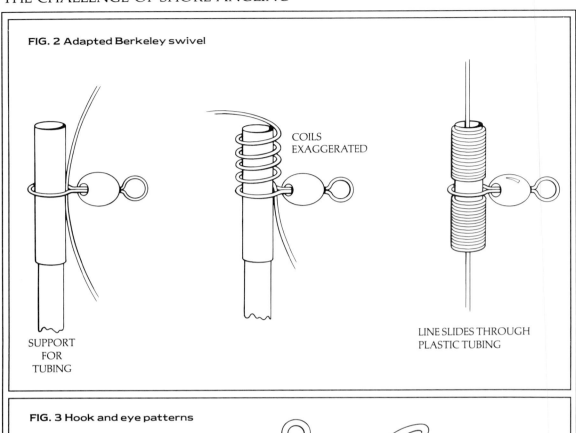

COILS
EXAGGERATED

SUPPORT
FOR
TUBING

LINE SLIDES THROUGH
PLASTIC TUBING

FIG. 3 Hook and eye patterns

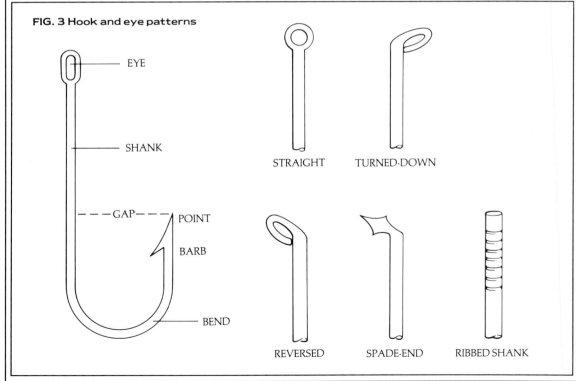

EYE

SHANK

GAP — POINT

BARB

BEND

STRAIGHT   TURNED-DOWN

REVERSED   SPADE-END   RIBBED SHANK

damage. A spade-end comes between the two in this respect. A turned-down eye is useful when fishing with live prawns and a reversed eye is useful for tandem rigs.

Length of shank is also important, in conjunction with the width of the gap between the point and shank. Long-shank, narrow-gap hooks are ideal for flatfish whereas a short-shank, wide-gap hook is useful for livebaiting. Generally the gap needs to be wide if you are going to fish a large, bulky bait. This will ensure that the point is clear and can be driven home on demand.

You should check that the point of your hook is short and sharp. A long point blunts easily and will require frequent honing with a whetstone.

In the chart below I have given a star rating to a few brands and sizes of hooks: * is fair, ** good and *** excellent.

Before leaving hooks I must stress that you do have to look after them. Keep them neatly sorted according to patterns and size, and separate from other items of tackle, and don't put them back without drying them first. Fine-wire hooks corrode very easily and their points constantly need

sharpening. Despite the robust appearance of stronger hooks, these are also subject to constant wear and tear. No matter what the hook, if you want it to do its job well then you must spend a little time cleaning, drying and sharpening.

BOOMS

The function of a boom is to hold the trace away from the main line and so prevent tangles. Unfortunately they are bulky and so reduce casting distances because of increased air resistance. But they can be useful where distance is not a priority or where the use of three bulky baits eliminates any pretence of finesse. Booms make tackling up very easy and, for example when dogfish- or whiting-fishing, present fish strips conveniently.

Over the years I have made and tested hundreds of booms, but nowadays stick to one basic pattern of home-made boom (Fig. 4). All you need to make one is some fine stainless wire or some slightly thicker galvanized wire, a 3 in (7.5 cm) round nail, a vice (unless you bang the nail into a piece of wood and pull it out after each boom is made), pliers and a screwdriver. Coil the wire tightly around the nail

CHOOSING HOOKS

MAKE AND/OR MODEL	PATTERN	STAR RATING	SIZE	APPLICATION
Mustad	3730A Aberdeen	**	6–1/0	Flatfish and small-to-medium bottom feeders
Mustad	3282 Aberdeen	*	6–1/0	As above
			2–4/0	Bass
			4/0–6/0	Rays and cod (be careful not to over-stress hook)
Au Lion D'or	1322 Aberdeen	**	6–1/0	As for 3730A
			2–4/0	Bass
			4/0–6/0	Rays and cod
Partridge	Z10 Aberdeen	***	8	Sole
			6–1/0	As for 3730A
			2–4/0	Bass
			4/0	Rays, cod
Breakaway	Spearpoint/spade	***		Hook packages graded according to species
Partridge	Z5 Flashpoint	**	6–4	Mackerel and garfish
			2–1/0	Pollack and wrasse
			2/0–4/0	Bass
			4/0–7/0	Conger and cod
Mustad	O'Shaughnessy	**	1–2/0	Bass, dogfish, wrasse
			3/0–7/0	Conger

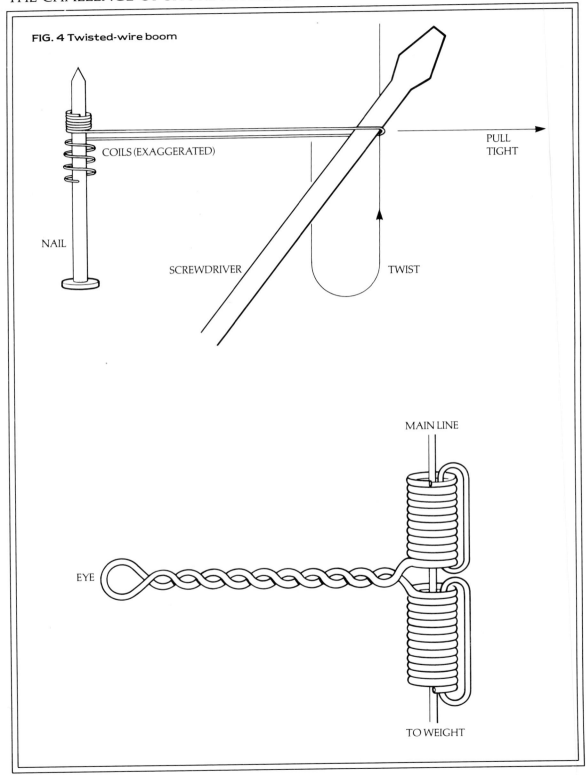

FIG. 4 Twisted-wire boom

COILS (EXAGGERATED)

PULL
TIGHT

NAIL

SCREWDRIVER

TWIST

MAIN LINE

EYE

TO WEIGHT

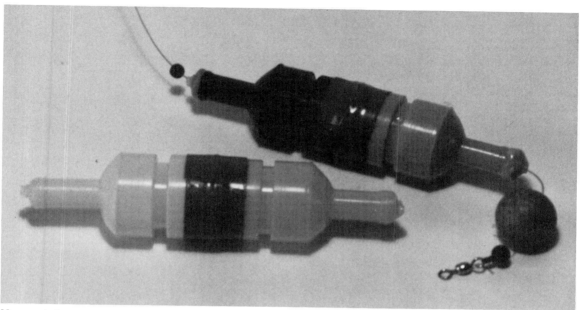

Home-made floats

for ten to twelve turns. Make a loop at the side, coil around the nail for a further ten to twelve turns and trim off. Put the screwdriver through the loop, pull tightly upon it and twist, removing the screwdriver at the last moment.

When the nail is removed you will have a twisted wire boom that can be secured to the main line without using any knots. To make sliding booms you repeat exactly the same process, but this time over a piece of plastic tubing that is supported by the nail.

If you don't want to make your own, Avis booms are good and commercial wire booms are available, usually made up into a pre-tied paternoster. However, these seem a bit expensive when you consider that you can make your own for under two pence a time!

FLOATS

My favourite floats are the slim West Country models. These are made of compacted polystyrene and slide freely on the line with the aid of a core of plastic tubing. They are available in a range of sizes and colours to suit each angler's particular requirements.

These floats are aerodynamic in shape and offer less resistance to a taking fish. However, their primary function is simply to suspend a bait in mid-water. Even so, there are many models to choose from, some quite clumsy and some very refined.

The angler who keeps his eyes open can make home-made floats from a variety of materials. Some of my favourites started life as the casings of party poppers. Instead of throwing these away with the various papers and crackers left after a Christmas dinner, I noticed that you could thread two shells together at the bottom and produce a reasonable float body. I then taped around the join and glued an empty ballpoint pen inserted lengthways through both shells to make them into sliding floats.

I used Araldite glue, securing the tubing firmly at both ends but taking care not to fill in the hole. Out of twelve discarded shells I quickly made six reasonable floats for a minimal cost in glue and a few pence for a packet of Bic plastic tubes (as supplied to carp anglers).

The floats function perfectly well and are very effective for both livebaiting and float-fishing for wrasse, mackerel and garfish. Nor are these the only floats that you can make quickly and cheaply.

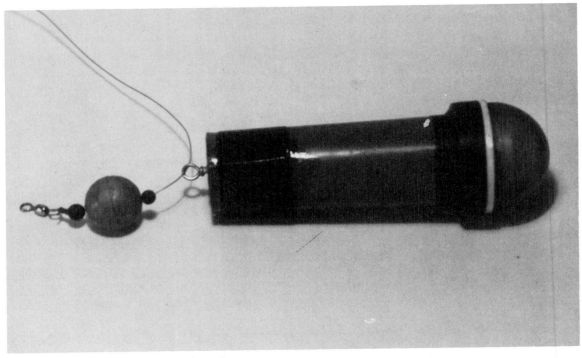

An electric float assembled out of inexpensive bits and pieces

Carefully drill lengthwise through a wine-bottle cork and glue in a plastic lining to make a small but effective instant float.

Night-fishing float

Floats can be as simple or as ingenious as you care to make them. I like to float-fish at night, and long ago discovered that you can still catch mackerel even in the dead of night. However, my eyesight is not good and so I was relying — even then with difficulty — on chemical aids attached to the float. I solved this problem by buying a child's Halloween torch, which takes 1 HP7 battery, some child's bubble mix, and a plastic egg and toy.

I padded the bubble container with foam and cut the middle out of the top. Into the container I put the torch. I then glued half of the clear plastic egg to the removable top of the container. A piece of bent stainless steel wire was glued and taped into position as an eye and the top replaced — with the torch on — and the container taped around the bottom both for security and to keep the water out.

The result was an electric float — costing under £1 — that stays clearly visible for 1¾ hours on a single HP7 battery. It is weighted by a ¾ oz (20 gm) drilled bullet and, with beads sliding to both sides of the eye, can be set to whatever depth you like.

When you want to change the battery you have only to remove the top and tape it together again. I am sure that there are many different ways to make such floats and would not be surprised if others had devised their own solution.

ROD RESTS AND BITE ALARMS

When you fish for any length of time it becomes much easier to place the rod on a rest and watch the tip than to continually hold it. Several varieties of rod rest are available. On the beach a sand spike can be used (a monopod that holds the rod erect and so keeps the line above crashing breakers), tripods are used for rock-fishing and there are even systems that bolt onto fishing boxes (such as the excellent taper-trak from MPH Associates) which are good for holding light float or similar rods.

I have used all of the above at one time or another, but for rock and estuary fishing I took the idea of the tripod a little further and produced a home-made variety that incorporated an electronic carp alarm and a visual drop-back indicator for slack-line bites. It is very efficient and quite simple to make, but does have its limitations in windy conditions.

If you look at the photograph you will see a 12 ft (3.6 m) beachcaster set up on a home-made tripod and Sundridge Buz 1 alarm. I use the Sundridge for a fixed-spool reel and the cheaper BJ alarm with multipliers. This is basically because the 'ears' of the alarms are different shapes and so are easier to erect with a particular type of reel.

Instead of constructing a straightforward tripod I ran a bank stick into a rectangle of wood measuring 2½ in × 3 in (6.5 cm × 7.5 cm) (Fig. 5). This is

necessary to take the alarm. To the front of the rectangle I attached the front legs of the tripod, using dowel, and strengthened them with a nylon cord in-between. I cut a U-shape out of the back of the wooden block and bolted the third leg so that it could swing in this recess. Again I used nylon cords from the back to front legs.

To the bank stick is taped a piece of rubber tubing, into which is threaded a section of straightened coathanger. On the end of this is secured some plastic tubing, a piece of polystyrene, a hairgrip and a drilled bullet weight. The holding power of the hairgrip in increased by the use of a piece of tight-fitting silicon rubber.

This is a visual drop-back indicator: if a fish picks up your bait and swims towards you the line will go slack. The alarm does not sound, but the grip, which is clipped to your line, falls and dramatically

Tripod and electronic alarm

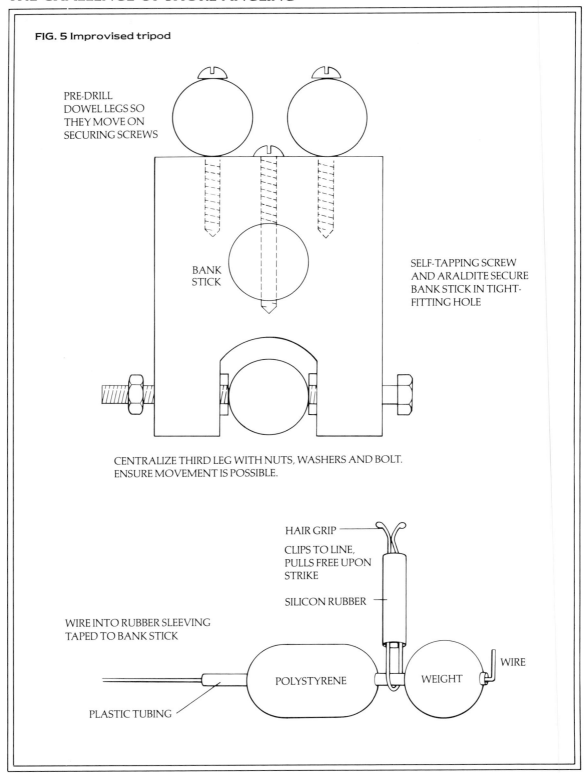

FIG. 5 Improvised tripod

PRE-DRILL DOWEL LEGS SO THEY MOVE ON SECURING SCREWS

BANK STICK

SELF-TAPPING SCREW AND ARALDITE SECURE BANK STICK IN TIGHT-FITTING HOLE

CENTRALIZE THIRD LEG WITH NUTS, WASHERS AND BOLT. ENSURE MOVEMENT IS POSSIBLE.

HAIR GRIP

CLIPS TO LINE, PULLS FREE UPON STRIKE

SILICON RUBBER

WIRE INTO RUBBER SLEEVING TAPED TO BANK STICK

POLYSTYRENE

WEIGHT

WIRE

PLASTIC TUBING

emphasizes the bite. Be sure to bend the end of the wire so that the weight does not fall off. In practise the tension of the line to your sinker will support the indicator. However, with a slack-line bite the tension is inadequate to support the weight and so the bite becomes clearly visible.

This tripod arrangement is ideal for some locations, including piers, although not all. I would not dream of using it on Dungeness beach but I do use it whenever I can, simply because I have found it very efficient and well worth the trouble to make.

Advances in tackle take place all the time, both in the re-emergence of old ideas in a new guise and in the form of completely new ideas. In the next chapter, which deals with casting, I shall take some of the ideas that I have discussed above and describe practical ways of using your tackle.

CHAPTER THREE

Casting

While there is little doubt that the ability to cast well is a valuable aid to successful fishing, it should be kept in perspective. It is a means of delivering your bait to the fish, in as good a condition as possible. If you want your tackle over 200 yards (180 m) from the shore, persevere and you will probably succeed. However, there is no point hurling out an empty hook. If you want distance then you must also not stint on your bait presentation. There are ways of getting the bait out safely, most of which are dealt with in the chapter on baits.

Nowadays the fascination with casting tournaments is turning this aspect of fishing into a sport in itself. Unfortunately there is also a negative side that is reflected in the attitudes of some of the people that I have met during fishing trips. They are sometimes embarrassed by their own casting compared with that of others, and on more than one occasion I have seen this feeling flare up into outright hostility. Sometimes this is because they cannot cast straight and so cause a tangle with another angler's tackle.

Ninety-nine times out of a hundred the average fisherman will put down a tangle to experience, but once in a while he will get angry. What is inexcusable — and unfortunately on the increase — is when the person who caused the tangle blames others. Distance must be accompanied by accuracy. There will be occasions when a lot of people choose to fish the same mark that you do. A good fisherman will be considerate, avoiding tangles and politely dealing with them when they occur, but he will also make sure that he does not inconvenience others by persistently casting, purposely or through incompetence, to where they were fishing first.

Starting to cast

Naturally, you cannot become proficient at casting overnight. If possible practise with a friend, each taking turns to cast while the other watches. This is important, as an onlooker will spot flaws in your casting style that you don't notice.

A common mistake is to rely solely on brute strength when casting. Although force does have its place, it usually leads to the line snapping or a much reduced distance. Style is more important than raw power. When you gain mastery over the style, you will gradually be able to apply more and more power. Finally your technique will be perfected, and you will enjoy total control over style, speed, power and timing.

Sea Angler magazine runs an excellent casting club with both voluntary and paid instructors, from time to time listing their names. Or write to the Editor, enclosing a stamped self-addressed envelope, to explain your difficulty. The instructors are all excellent casters and have kindly volunteered their time and expertise to help other anglers. If you contact your local instructor you should also find him friendly and both willing and able to help.

Before moving on to casting styles let us look briefly at the tackle tuning that should be carried out beforehand. This topic is dealt with in terms of the two main types of reel.

Fixed-spools

On some models the bale arm is prone to accidentally trip during casting, leading to a crack-

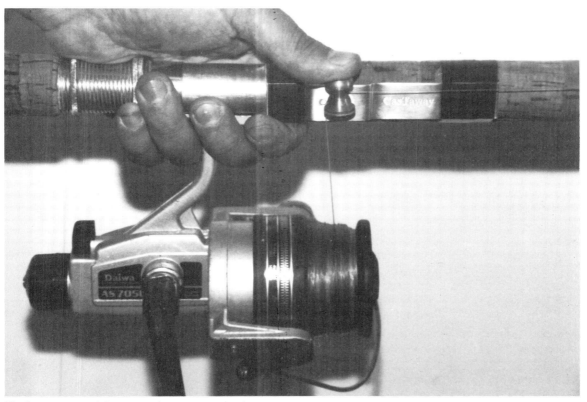

The Castaway, a simple but effective device for increasing distance of cast, unfortunately no longer manufactured

off (the line breaks) or an abortive cast. If your reel displays this tendency it is best to deal with it immediately. In some cases this can be accomplished by tightening the tension that controls the bale arm release. In others it becomes necessary to remove the wire with a hacksaw, leaving just the roller assembly to distribute the line (Fig. 6). This cures the problem but it does devalue the reel for resale.

With a fixed-spool the line is held against the rod until the moment of release. However, the heavier the weight you are using, the more difficult this becomes. Frequently the line slips free too early in the cast, reducing distance. To overcome this problem there are three alternatives, two shop-bought and one home-made.

The photograph shows a device known as the Castaway, glued and taped to the handle of a beachcaster. Unfortunately now only available second-hand, the Castaway worked on a slightly different principle to other devices that are marketed today. The line was wrapped around a swivelling capstan which was then held in place during the cast by the angler's thumb. At the critical moment the angler lifted his thumb and the line peeled away.

Using the Castaway, you were able to exert full power during the cast. However, it was essential that a leader was used as the line was locked down so hard that incorrect timing of the release would almost invariably result in a crack-off. It will be interesting to see if a comparably effective product comes on the market.

Another device is the Breakaway thumb button, which is widely available in tackle shops. This is attached to the rod handle directly over the reel and is also secured by the angler's thumb. A button is depressed which traps the line. At the critical

FIG. 6 Modification of bale arm

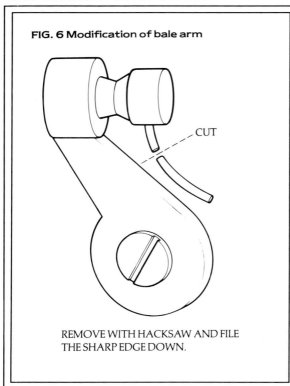

CUT

REMOVE WITH HACKSAW AND FILE
THE SHARP EDGE DOWN.

FIG. 7 Underfilled spool

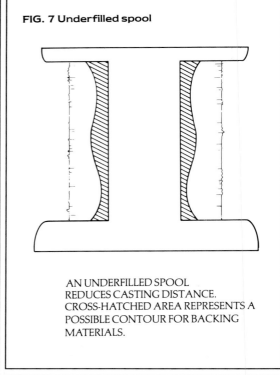

AN UNDERFILLED SPOOL
REDUCES CASTING DISTANCE.
CROSS-HATCHED AREA REPRESENTS A
POSSIBLE CONTOUR FOR BACKING
MATERIALS.

FIG. 8 Correctly filled spool

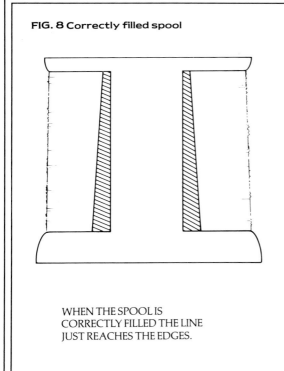

WHEN THE SPOOL IS
CORRECTLY FILLED THE LINE
JUST REACHES THE EDGES.

FIG. 9 Overfilled spool

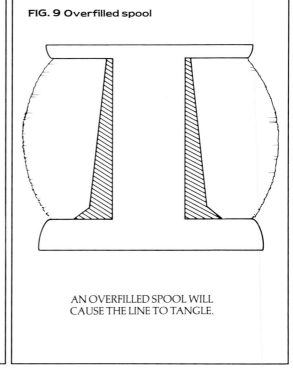

AN OVERFILLED SPOOL WILL
CAUSE THE LINE TO TANGLE.

moment in the cast, the thumb is lifted and the line is then free to peel smoothly off the reel. The idea is simple and works relatively well.

A third method is the fixing to the rod of a leather strap. This is folded over the line to hold it during the casting, but is then released at the right moment. The disadvantage of this method is that the leather may dangle and interfere with the line coming off the spool, which brings me to another point.

When you fill a fixed-spool the line will be laid in a noticeable pattern. Quite often there will be a bulge top and bottom with a dip in-between. Ideally it should be cone-shaped and to achieve this you will need to build up layers of backing material and waterproof tape (Figs. 7–9).

Multipliers

These require finer tuning than fixed-spools. They undergo a great deal of stress and need frequent attention to keep the edge to their performance. Neglect can lead to serious problems.

Sand can work into the frame, leading to damage if not washed clear almost immediately. Similarly, corrosion is accelerated by salt water, causing further damage if left unattended. These two factors combine to mean that multipliers require regular cleaning and lubrication.

Lubrication is particularly important. The density of the oil used will not only allow the reel to continue to function but will also affect its casting performance. Too thick and the reel will run slowly, reducing distance. Too light and inadequate protection is afforded, some multipliers running too fast and still requiring extra braking. This tendency can be countered by increasing the thickness of the oil until you reach a point where the reel runs properly.

It should be noted that this additional braking is purely a refinement of the reel's performance. The greatest part of the work should be done by the reel itself. In the light of this many people have experimented with single oils and mixtures. The most popular, from light to thick, are SAE30, SAE90, or STP if the former prove to be too thin. If by any chance these are too thick, you may find it necessary to experiment with 10/50 engine oil.

On a different note, the spool may occasionally slip from beneath your thumb, normally causing a burn. Also, the leader knot may catch on your skin and cut it. To avoid the former, Breakaway have developed a device called a Thumbrake. To avoid the latter, simply watch the line as you reel in the last lengths and ensure that the knot is wound to either the extreme right or the extreme left of the spool.

The Thumbrake clips to the rear bar of the reel frame. It has a rubber band wound around both it and the rod that stretches as the angler presses the rubber pad of the device onto the spool. At the moment of release the angler removes his thumb and the rubber band whips it away. It is comfortable to use and fairly modest thumb pressure holds the spool locked.

I have found that the Thumbrake works better if used in conjunction with a trigger whipped to the rod. The band stretches tighter and the trigger helps the angler to keep a firmer grip. Use hair bands (the sort used for pony tails) instead of plain rubber, as they last much longer.

The trigger itself is easily made by bending the last half inch (1.25 cm) of a tough 2½ in (6.5 cm) strip of aluminium at ninety degrees to the rest. This leaves plenty of space for the whipping. Attach your multiplier to the beachcaster and experiment with positions for the trigger until you find the place, over and above the reel seat, where it feels most comfortable. Tape it temporarily in position and then whip it securely.

Whipping

This is a simple method of securing rod rings to the blank (Figs. 10–13). You need whipping thread, a 6 in (15 cm) loop of nylon monofilament (of at least 12 lb/5.5 Kg b.s.) and some good rod varnish. Simply coil the thread about the blank, trapping the end under the first turn and then burying it as you wind the thread tightly around the blank, leaving no space between each coil. As the coils mount you will approach the point at which the whipping is to finish. A quarter of an inch (0.5 cm) before your destination, lay the loop of nylon alongside, ends towards the whipping already in place, and whip over this as well.

When you reach the point at which you want to

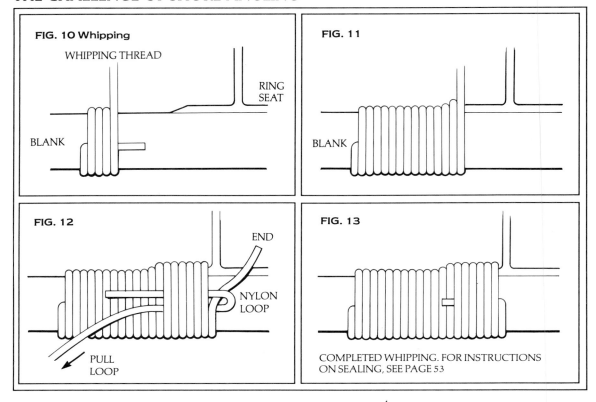

FIG. 10 Whipping
WHIPPING THREAD
RING SEAT
BLANK

FIG. 11
BLANK

FIG. 12
END
NYLON LOOP
PULL LOOP

FIG. 13
COMPLETED WHIPPING. FOR INSTRUCTIONS ON SEALING, SEE PAGE 53

stop, simply cut the thread above where you are holding it and pass the end through the nylon loop. Grasp the ends of the nylon firmly and pull it so that the thread is pulled under its own coils. Pull this as tight as you can and trim carefully with a razor blade, cutting the thread as close to the whipping as possible.

Now that all the preparations for casting have been dealt with, let us look at the main styles, specifically the off-the-ground cast and the pendulum cast. As far as the first is concerned, I am not going to confuse anybody with a plethora of instructions for what is, after all, basically very simple. Instead consider the sequence of diagrams which, together with the brief explanation, will guide the beginner through the whole procedure.

The pendulum cast is more complicated, depending as much on speed as on power, and reflecting instantly any flaws in the angler's style. A smooth action is essential, particularly when casting with a multiplier. Any jerkiness will show itself in shortened distance, crack-offs or bird's nests. The most important thing for a novice is to get the action right before trying to maximize the power.

The cast
Use the following instructions in conjunction with Figs. 15–18.

Place your hands comfortably on the handle of the rod, ensuring that your grasp on the reel and/or line is secure. Place the toes of your left foot so that they face in the direction in which you are going to cast. Put the right foot about 6 in (15 cm) behind the left and turn it outwards so that it is at ninety degrees to the left.

From the top of the rod let out sufficient line so that the weight has a 7 ft (2 m) drop. Twist your body clockwise until just before you start to feel discomfort. Put your weight on the right leg and hold the rod up, with the reel moving into a position just above eye level. Both arms should be comfortably extended and the weight allowed to settle directly below the rod tip. The chest will be

Casting for cod; the feet at 90° to each other, knees bent at the beginning of the sweep

FIG. 14 Off-the-ground cast

Pull the rod upwards until the left hand is at shoulder height and some 16 in (40 cm) away from chest. Swivel the torso while transferring weight from your right foot to the left.

The left arm pulls the rod butt across the chest and takes it to the left hip. Simultaneously the right arm pushes straight out in the direction of the cast, the angler's body completing the swivel movement of torso and leaning into the cast.

The weight is allowed free flight at the split second after the right arm has been fully extended and the rod tip is pointing straight at the target.

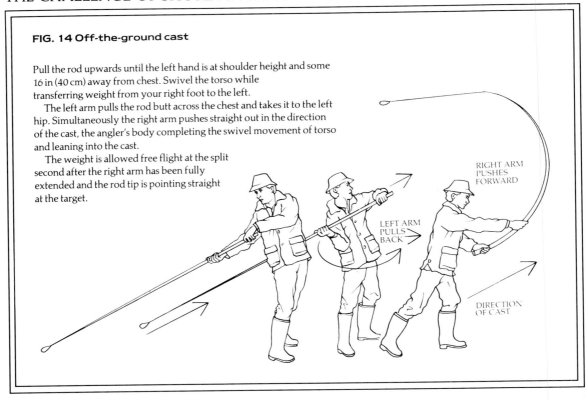

RIGHT ARM PUSHES FORWARD

LEFT ARM PULLS BACK

DIRECTION OF CAST

facing in the opposite direction to that of the cast.

Push the rod tip downwards to make the weight swing in an arc. Stop the rod from descending too far but allow the weight to swing upwards until it rises above eye level. When it reaches the top of its arc pull the rod back, using the blank to guide the weight so that it travels to the right of the blank and swings high in the air behind your right shoulder. You will feel a split-second pause as the weight reaches its maximum height and checks before the descent.

In that split second sweep the rod to the position at which you would begin the off-the-ground cast — or at least begin the sweep. The weight will be following the rod tip and should be travelling at sufficient velocity to avoid contact with the ground. Thus when you enter the push/pull movement (the 'power stroke') you will not only have the power from the final stage behind it, but also the momentum that the pendulum has gathered.

It is crucial that you do not hit the ground in the final swing through and around. If you do then the rod tip has been lowered too far or there was not a long enough drop of line between the tip and the weight. If the weight does hit the ground considerable distance may be lost.

If at any point in the cast you feel that you want to abort it and try again, just drop the rod tip. The weight will hit the ground, bounce and stay there. Stay calm, try again and keep practising until you get it right.

Some of the problems encountered with the pendulum are caused by the angler's lack of speed or sense of balance. To gain full compression, the rod tip needs to travel through a full 360 degree rotation. Sometimes this is not possible, either because the angler does not have sufficient control, or because the fishing location is crowded — say, when casting from a popular pier.

Being a bit on the bulky side, I tend to be too slow to make full and effective use of the pendulum. Eventually, I borrowed from this and other casting styles to develop a simple technique that compensates for my lack of speed.

FIG. 15 Pendulum cast

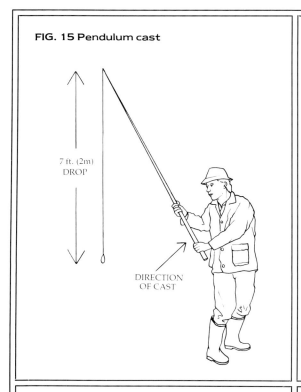

7 ft. (2m)
DROP

DIRECTION
OF CAST

FIG. 16

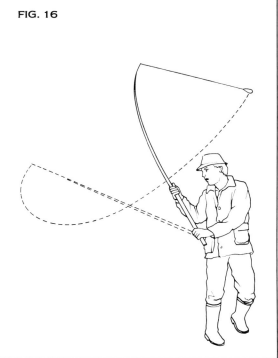

FIG. 17

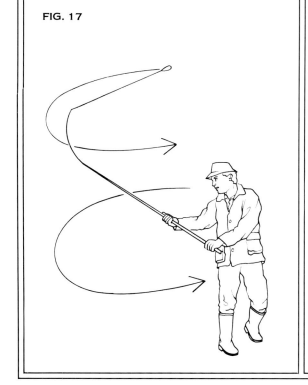

FIG. 18

During the power stroke
transfer your weight from
the right leg to the left as
you step forward, leaning
into the cast.

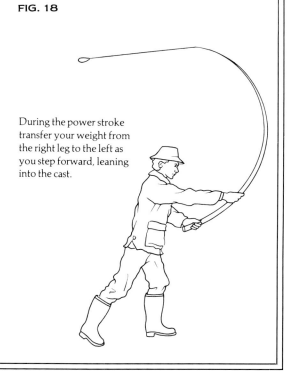

The cast begins in the same way as the pendulum, but with the drop between the tip and the sinker much reduced, to about three to four feet. I start by swinging the lead gently backwards and then letting it swing forward and up.

Just before it reaches the maximum height I push it backwards again, swivelling the torso slightly so that the weight reaches further behind. As it swings forward again, I work the rod with greater effort and speed. The third time it goes back is the last: when the lead is fully extended behind me I bring it forward and round, swivelling the torso back to true and going straight into the power stroke of the cast, which is identical to the final stages of the pendulum.

I use this cast for nearly every situation. It's not going to win any awards for distance, but it will put the tackle out more than 125 yards without bursting a blood vessel or spiking an observer. It is easy to practise, and gives you the security of always being in control. The only thing you have to guard against is that the swivelling motion can cause the cast to veer off to the left. To counter this, all you have to do is to watch your footing in the first stages, pointing the leading foot slightly to the right and adjusting your stance accordingly.

CHAPTER FOUR

Baits and their Presentation

I am often surprised by the number of people who spend a lot of money on tackle, but who neglect the standard of their bait. This is a great pity as poor-quality bait drastically reduces the chance of success.

If he takes the trouble to obtain first-class bait, the angler may be agreeably surprised by the difference it makes. Unfortunately such bait is often not obtainable from tackle shops. With the exception of frozen squid or fresh herring, many bought offerings suffer from the treatment that they receive or the length of time that it takes to get them to the retailer. All too often a wrapped package of ragworm turns out to be pitiful in size and all but lifeless.

To avoid disappointment, many anglers are prepared to devote the necessary time to collecting their own bait, which gives them a much wider choice. For example, prawns can be deadly but are seldom stocked, and the same applies to razorfish, sea slaters and hermit crabs.

In this chapter I will describe ways of both gathering bait and presenting it. I have made a selection of 14 of the most successful baits, including a couple of the better exotics.

When deciding to go for a particular species of fish you will find it essential to know what baits attract it. Bearing this in mind I have compiled a table of 14 target species and graded the baits suitable, in my experience, for each.

RAGWORM

There are several species of ragworm, although only a few are used as bait. The most useful are king, silver and harbour ragworm. Of the three, the king ragworm attains the greatest size, specimens being recorded of over 2 ft (60 cm) long. This, with their widespread distribution, makes them a very popular bait.

King and harbour ragworm both favour tidal areas where the bottom is composed of thick mud or a mud and gravel mixture. The best worms are often to be found in those sections of beach that are still partially waterlogged. Ragworm don't like a parched environment. When you consider that these worms are predators, then the reason becomes obvious. Their chance of a meal may often depend on the speed with which they can tunnel, and they do this faster in wet mud than in dry.

The bait-digger should equip himself with reliable wellingtons and a good fork. Check that the fork handle is secure and not rotted. If it is even slightly suspect you will find that a gravel and mud mixture invariably highlights any weaknesses. Several methods of digging for ragworm have been used in the past, depending on the worms' abundance or scarcity. If the surface of the mud is peppered with tiny holes, the chances are that it abounds with tiny harbour ragworm. If the holes are larger, some being roughly ¼ in (0.5 cm) in diameter, king rag are also present or you have stumbled across a bed of cockles.

If the worms are obviously plentiful it may be worthwhile digging a trench. Start just clear of your target area and gradually work your way through and around, putting any worms in a container with some dry seaweed. Try not to break any, and reject them if you do. If you come across any worms that are full of green fluid put those back as well. If you mix them with healthy worms pretty soon your entire stock will be ruined.

Preparation of worms

At the end of your dig carefully wash the worms and lay them on clean newspaper. This will begin the process of drying and toughening them. When you get home the paper will be waterlogged and will need to be changed. When you do this, start by turning the edge of a clean sheet of newspaper over three times, each fold being approximately 1½ in (4 cm). Lay a couple of worms side by side and fold the paper over the two, unless they are very large, in which case wrap just one. Repeat this procedure until you have wrapped ten worms. Fold over the ends of the package and tape them down, also sticking down the loose edge.

Worms kept in this fashion stay healthy for a couple of days, provided that they are left in a cool place. The fridge is ideal, though it may be too cold near the freezer compartment. Alternatively, instead of wrapping them up you can just tip all of the worms into a bucket of dry peat, digging them out just before you go fishing. This really toughens them up.

Another method of keeping ragworm alive is to have an efficient aquarium. This should be equipped with an under-gravel filter and slightly cooled. Salt water that is placed inside is aerated for a week to settle the environment. Only then can you add any worms. Once these are settled in you should keep a close eye on them. If any appear sickly remove them from the tank, taking care to keep your hands out of the water as much as possible. For a 3 ft (1 m) tank the maximum number of worms would be around fifty.

Similar methods may be used to preserve silver or white ragworm. However, these worms are obtained from different environments, as they prefer clean sand to the muddier haunts of their larger brethren. Silver ragworm are firm-bodied and lively. Their attractiveness to fish has made them legendary in match-fishing circles. Unfortunately they are not plentiful and so, unless you stumble on a bed while digging for lugworm, they can be difficult to find. Many people keep such locations among their closest secrets. If you can get a friend to divulge the whereabouts of a bed of silver rag, you will greatly improve your chances of catching many species of fish.

Baiting

There are two methods of baiting with ragworm: tail-first or head-first. The former results in a more secure bait for casting while the latter produces a more attractive bait as part of the tail dangles behind the bend of the hook. For hard casting I always stick to the first method as the second may lead to bits of the worm being torn from the hook.

As a last point, when you dig for ragworm or anything else, be sure to backfill the holes that you have made behind you. Also, check the size of the worms that you have dug, as very small ones are useless for almost everything except tiny flatfish or mullet. Don't take what you will not use. If anglers are conservation-minded about bait the supply will last much longer.

LUGWORM

These worms are common around British shores, and are often found on beaches in vast colonies. They are less choosy than ragworm about habitat, living not only in sand but also in mud or mud and grit environments. Their bodies are very soft and easily damaged, the soft flesh being connected to a tube that is filled with sand.

A tell-tale sign of the presence of a lugworm is a cast — a tube of sand rising in a coil. Close by there is often a breathing hole and between this and the cast will be a U-shaped tube, which is where the lugworm will be found.

When digging for individual worms, map out in your mind's eye where the middle of the bend will lie. Then start digging far enough back so that you don't stab or break the worm. Alternatively you can use a lugworm pump, such as the Colpat model, which can descend nearly 2 ft (60 cm) in the sand within seconds. These pumps extract a cylinder of sand in which the lugworm will often be found.

Lugworm are best used immediately, although they may keep for a while if wrapped in the same way as ragworm. However, it is best if only one worm is included in each fold of paper, so that there are two thicknesses around it instead of one.

Baiting

When you come to use the worms, it is best if you have a selection of long-shanked hooks and suit the

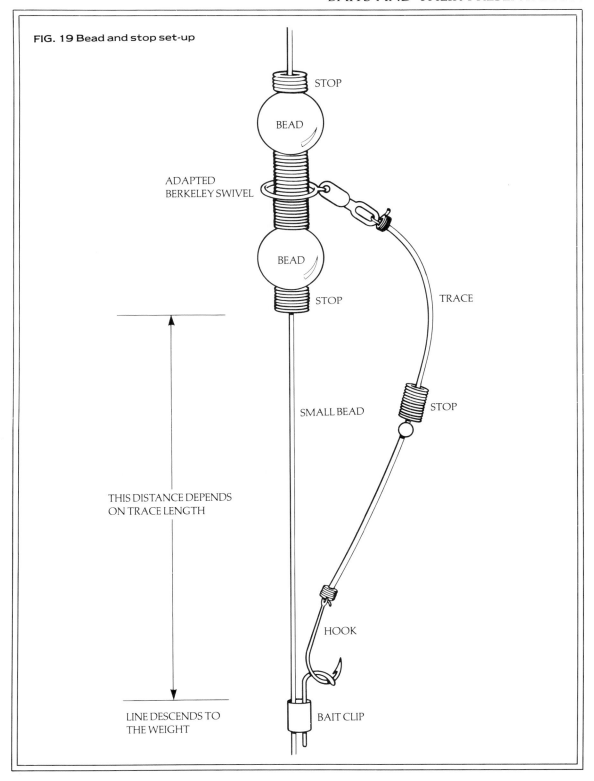

FIG. 19 Bead and stop set-up

STOP

BEAD

ADAPTED
BERKELEY SWIVEL

BEAD

STOP

TRACE

SMALL BEAD

STOP

THIS DISTANCE DEPENDS
ON TRACE LENGTH

HOOK

LINE DESCENDS TO
THE WEIGHT

BAIT CLIP

hook size and number of worms used to the fish that you are after. For example, for cod you might thread five or even six lugworms on a Mustad 3282 size 6/0 Aberdeen, working the first worms over the eye and up the trace. But for dabs you might use a single lugworm on a size 6 Aberdeen.

If you want to use a bait clip for casting, so as to streamline your tackle and decrease air resistance, it is a good idea to add a bead and stop to the trace (Fig. 19). This is important as it prevents air resistance pushing the worm up the trace and away from the hook. Bait clips are easily made by bending over the end of a piece of wire. A short section of rubber sleeving is threaded over the wire and the line, leaving the bend free for securing the hook during casting.

Stops can also be made very easily, particularly if you are friendly with a telephone engineer. If he has any waste pieces of telephone cable you can remove the fine inner wires, coil the cable about a nail and slide it off. Cut it into ¼ in (0.5 cm) spirals. To use, simply thread a spiral on the line, hold one end tightly and twist. The tubing will elongate and form a very secure grip on the nylon monofilament.

Fig. 19 shows the bead and stop set-up. The trace for the hook is shown in a typical paternoster set-up. The main benefit is that the tackle is streamlined to reduce the effect of air resistance. A drawback is that worm baits are exposed to the full force of the cast, resulting in them being pushed up the trace, but the bead and stop will minimize this problem.

PRAWNS

These can be a deadly bait, probably because of their very quick, erratic movements. When prawns are suspended on float tackle there are few predators that will turn them down. However, if dead, their attraction pales considerably.

Prawns have quite fragile bodies, and this should be allowed for in the style of casting. It is useless hurling out your tackle with such force that the cast tears the prawn from the hook. As a result the distance that can be achieved is severely limited. Concentrate on fishing well at short distance, sacrificing range for the confidence brought by the use of excellent bait. Your approach will in any case be determined by the type of fish that you are after.

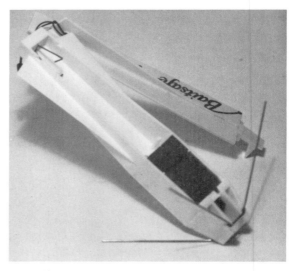

An Intakl baitsafe

With some species, notably pollack and wrasse, distance is not a factor.

Although I rarely use prawns for legering, there are occasions when they can be most useful. A specific example is the use of a big prawn to take thornback ray. However, here you again face the question of distance. Fortunately you can now buy a handy device called an Intakl Baitsafe. This acts as a weight and storage compartment during casting. It opens on hitting the water and releases the prawn, which can then operate effectively in an area where the number of crabs would render worm baits or fish strip all but useless. It is a good alternative tactic.

Gathering prawns

Prawns can be gathered in several ways. But note first of all that for keeping them alive a portable aerator is an essential piece of equipment and should be used from the very moment of capture. If you leave prawns, even for only a couple of hours, without aeration, you find that a considerable number have died.

The most popular method of collecting prawns is to use a drop-net, which you can either buy or make yourself. A piece of fish is placed in the net and secured to its bottom. Some anglers even pour pilchard oil over the fish. The net is lowered into the water and left on the seabed for a while to tempt

Searching for prawns — note the aerator to keep them alive

prawns to enter and investigate the chance of a snack. The net is then hauled smoothly and swiftly to the surface, the prawns are removed and the net is lowered once more.

Drop-netting is particularly good in summer but very limited in winter, which is a shame as prawns are an excellent bait for large whiting. The usual places to drop-net are harbour walls, pier stanchions, jetties or indeed almost any rocky mark into deep water.

Commercial prawn traps can be purchased and left overnight. Their main disadvantage is their vulnerability to theft, but used with buoys from a small boat this problem can be overcome.

During the summer, another successful method is to wade around the edges of rocks, pushing a long-handled net into and along every ledge and crack that you can find. Often you will catch some very large prawns. With a plastic bag tied at your waist, preferably with a bit of kelp in it, you will not have to keep stopping and going back for a bucket. You will simply need to empty the bag from time to time and put the prawns into the aerator.

A last method, and one which children adore, is to hunt through the rockpools with a small shrimping net. By turning over rocks you should come across some prawns. Place the net in the water behind the prawn, guide it slowly into the net and

The Colpat pump in operation

remove the net from the water. Don't rush or the prawn will become alarmed and take off at high speed.

Baiting

To bait with prawns, insert the point of the hook into the third segment from the tail, moving it from the bottom and out of the top. Hooked in this manner, the prawn is still capable of lively motion. Do not hook it anywhere else as this will impede its movement.

Smaller prawns and shrimps can be used in bunches on a hook, but I don't recommend it on the grounds of conservation. An exception is if you use a push-net for gathering sand shrimps on a beach. The bigger of these make an excellent bait for whiting.

To store prawns for a long period of time, you will find that they can be kept in an aquarium without any ill effect. For those with little time for collection, one trip can serve several fishing sessions. Set the fish tank up as for ragworm, but do not put in more than about 20 prawns for every two gallons (9 l) of water.

PEELER CRABS

During the life-cycle of the common, shore or green crab, the crustacean sheds its shell several times. The same is true of edible and swimming crabs, although you should note that it is illegal to take edible crabs during the peeling period.

A crab carries its skeleton on the outside. Therefore to grow it develops a new, soft shell beneath the old. During this time, when it is known as a peeler crab, it is a superb bait for many species of fish. When the new shell is ready, the crab discards its old external skeleton and seeks cover until its new shell has hardened. Quite often you will find soft-backed crabs, but generally the harder the shell the less the crab's potential as bait.

To tell if a crab is a peeler, examine the underneath of the joints on its legs or claws. These may be

A male crab clutches a peeling female

several colours, though not at the same time. If they are colourless, the crab is not a peeler. Red joints indicate that the new shell is just forming and the crab is not yet usable, while brown or black joints identify a peeler as ready for use.

The most prolific area for crabs is one that combines rocks, for cover, with plenty of weed and mud to bury themselves in. Estuaries provide ideal habitats while rockpools on the beach are also worth investigating. Spring usually sees the start of the moulting period, the process accelerating as the water temperature rises.

As you hunt through likely places you may come across a larger crab tightly clutching a smaller one. The latter will be a female crab that has sought the male's protection during the peeling process. It will usually be either a perfect peeler or a very soft-backed crab.

Baiting

To bait with peeler crab, leave them alive until you actually need them and then kill them humanely, with a sharp knock on the head. Remove the claws and legs, peeling the shells from the soft flesh underneath. The claws and legs make excellent bait for flatfish. Peel the body and hook it right through from the top, running the point in and out of one of the leg sockets. For hard casting tie the bait round with elasticated thread. This often makes the bait virtually unrecognizable as a crab, but does not seem to deter fish in the slightest.

Hermit Crabs

These carry a shell on their backs, into which they retreat if threatened or disturbed. Left alone, they will recover from their fright and amble ponderously along the bottom, looking for food and using their comparatively large claws to grab it. The shells are donated by various other animals, whelks in particular being favoured by the young.

Hermit crabs can grow fairly large — and it is these that make the best bait. They live by scavenging on marine debris, discarding their shells for bigger ones as they outgrow them. During the time in which they leave one shell and enter another they are vulnerable.

The body is a soft, fluid-filled member with hooks and a strong muscle at the end. The hooks are wrapped around the extreme inside of the shell. If danger threatens, the muscle contracts and the body, using the anchorage of the hooks, is pulled inside the shell and out of danger.

To collect hermits from the shore you really need a drop-net. Lower it to the seabed and leave it, baited with a piece of fish, for about 20 minutes. It is then retrieved and the catch examined. Usually a heaving mass of crabs appear, along with a few prawns and one or two hermits. The prawns and the hermits are useful, but the other crabs are useless for everything except smoothhound and wrasse. There will not be any peelers as crabs don't eat during the moulting process.

Alternatively you can pay someone in a crabbing boat to collect the hermits that he finds in the crab pots. Most crab-catchers are quite happy to do this for a fee.

Once you have caught your hermits you have to get them out of their shells. Despite some enthusiastic advocacy to the contrary, this does not involve the unrestrained use of a hammer — an approach guaranteed to ruin the greater part of your bait. Far more effective is to heat the end of the shell with a lighter. As hermits are extremely susceptible to heat, they either vacate the shell immediately or perish, when they can be extracted with ease.

Baiting

To attach a hermit to the hook, pass the point through the muscle at the top and then between and out of the claws and legs. Never pierce the body as the fluids are lost immediately. For hard casting you will need to wrap the bait in soluble plastic, such as carp anglers use and which is available from many tackle shops.

SEA SLATERS

These little creatures strongly resemble a wood louse, except that they can grow much larger. They are also faster, scuttling away with surprising speed. Search for them in rocks that lie above the high-tide mark. Alternatively you can smoke some out from cracks in harbour or pier walls.

Concrete piers can sometimes come alive at night with sea slaters. Babbacombe Pier in Torbay abounds with them. However, they do like to be just above the water line, so don't take any chances when you collect them. Keep them alive in a bucket with some damp kelp in it and don't kill them until you come to use them. Two or three mounted on a hook are excellent bait for wrasse and whiting. Thread the point through the creature from underneath, taking care not to hit any vital organs.

SQUID

Two main types of squid are available to anglers: the small, pink-fleshed calamari and its larger relation, which has firm, white flesh. Both species have a thin layer of unpleasant black skin that should be removed for best results.

The larger squid, often obtainable from fishmongers as well as tackle shops, can be cut into tapering slices. It is tough and ideal for casting. To hook it, simply pass the point through one end of the strip. It will then flutter enticingly in the current. Many species respond to this, including mackerel, garfish, dogfish, whiting, bream, pollack and gurnard.

Calamari can also be cut into strips, but they are best fished whole on the bottom for conger, cod or bass. The tentacles, if two or three are threaded on a small hook, make good baits for gurnard or dabs.

A similar bait to squid, and just as effective, is the cuttlefish. These are often caught in crab pots, but during the summer they may also be caught from the shore on float tackle. Mackerel bait is used to attract them, but a treble hook should be tied to the bend of the main hook. When a cuttlefish takes the bait the float will descend slowly. However, striking will set the trailing treble into the cuttlefish.

Ashore they can be humanely killed and either frozen for future use or used immediately. Cuttlefish strip is particularly good for float-fishing for mackerel, garfish and pollack.

A catch of mackerel taken inside Brixham harbour

MACKEREL

During the summer these brightly coloured fish are easily caught from the shore. They give excellent sport, but are also valuable bait. Many species of fish are tempted by a well-displayed strip of mackerel, from dogfish right through to bass, tope and conger. Methods of catching mackerel are dealt with under their own chapter, but for now I will concentrate upon their use as bait.

Ideally, mackerel should be used either fresh or frozen within a few hours of capture. If you intend to use them from a fishmonger then a quick word of warning: it is not usually in your best interest to tell the assistant that you will be using them for bait. Also, most mackerel bought from such a source are often very soft and well past the condition in which they are most useful.

Freshness is essential. If you catch a mackerel, freeze it within six or so hours of capture and then use it for bait next to a chap using mackerel bought from the slab. You will almost certainly find that you have considerably more bites. It will also stand up to casting much better and can be sliced more easily from the carcass.

Baiting

To bait with mackerel there are really two choices, both according to the species sought. One is to take a complete fillet — or indeed a whole fish — for larger predators, the other to slice the flesh into neat, tapering strips, perfect for other mackerel and such species as garfish, bream, dogfish, gurnard and whiting. If you are using a strip or a long fillet, try hooking the bait through once, and once only, working the hook through the skin and out of the flesh. In this way there will be little twist when you retrieve and the bait will respond to the motion provided by the current to best advantage.

The liver and intestines should not be ignored as these can be very attractive to bass and grey mullet. The eyes hold a great attraction for pout, while a whole head, especially with trailing intestines, can be a useful conger bait.

Small strips are most frequently used on float tackle, when it is advisable to carefully strip any surplus flesh. This presents a neater bait and appears to be taken with more confidence, perhaps because the mackerel are fooled into mistaking the strip for a small fish.

For maximum economy, prepare the bait in the following way. Take a sharp knife and make an incision to both sides of the dorsal fin, starting just behind the head and finishing at the tail. Turn the fish over and do the same at the bottom. Place the mackerel on a firm surface and draw the knife down the flanks, separating the flesh into rectangular strips approximately ½ in (1.25 cm) wide. When the strips start to become too small, turn the knife and draw it from the last strip to the tail, separating the last part into two strips lengthways along the body.

Lift the end of these last two strips and draw off two long, tapering slices. These are ideal for scad, also known as horse mackerel. Then turn the knife and, carefully using the tip of the blade, separate the rest of the strips from the body. Turn the fish over and do the other side.

If using these strips on a sunny day place them in a covered container out of the sun. This will keep the flies off and prevent the strips drying out. The carcass should be disposed of, but you could mince it up and use the flesh as groundbait, perhaps mixing it with some dried breadcrumbs to produce a cloud effect. This could be further enhanced with the use of dried/powdered milk. If you spoon the mixture into the area where you are fishing you might well be agreeably surprised at the result.

SANDEELS

Five species of sandeels inhabit British waters, but those most familiar to British anglers are the lesser and greater sandeels, the latter often being referred to as launce. The lesser sandeel tends to stay closer inshore than its larger relation and often forms the bulk of those sandeels that are offered for sale. Sandeels can be found buried in the sand just above the low-tide line, timing their arrival in May and their departure in September by the water temperature.

A method of collecting sandeels which requires both skill and co-ordination involves the use of a special hook attached to a handle. The angler wades through the water, dragging the hook across the bottom. If an eel is caught it is swept to the surface and neatly captured by the angler. The method does work but you need to be quick, grabbing the eel before it can wriggle its way to freedom.

They can also be dug just above the low-tide line by cutting a long, shallow trench rather than a deep hole. Another method is to foulhook them with a string of small treble hooks tied on the line above a small weight. This seems to work best from harbour walls and piers, the sort of place where sandeels congregate year after year.

Whichever method of collection is used, care should be taken with the storage of live sandeels. Proper aeration is an essential factor. Whenever possible try to store them in the sea itself: a perforated covered plastic container, tied to the pier and thrown in, is ideal for this purpose.

Baiting

To bait without impairing the sandeel's natural liveliness is actually quite simple. You pass the hook through its mouth and out of the gills, turning the point to nick it lightly through the skin at the belly. Some people simply hook the fish through the back, just behind the head.

Sandeels can be used dead, although they are not nearly so successful. However, strips are often good for mackerel, garfish and scad. A disadvantage of sandeels in general is that the soft flesh tears easily. In the case of a whole sandeel this problem may be easily countered by a knot securing the tail to the trace. With a strip this is not possible, and the method of casting must be altered. A gentle lob will land the bait intact, whereas a high-pressure cast will rip the bait from the hook. Once again it is a question of balancing distance against the bait's tendency to disintegrate and the species sought.

RAZORFISH

These are shellfish with long, cigar-shaped shells. The two portions of the shell are held shut by a tough muscle running along the membranous hinge. The coloration is normally blue and white.

Razorfish are to be found on sandy beaches, close to the extreme of low water. As they are only uncovered for short periods of time there are comparatively few to collect. The greatest numbers are found during abnormally high spring tides, when more are exposed than usual.

There is no shortage of razorfish, and you have only to take a walk along the beach after a storm to confirm this. If you arrive right after a storm you will often find large numbers washed up and these can be frozen for future use. Quite often this is also an excellent time to fish as the abundance of food attracts fish in greater quantities than usual, tempting them to gorge.

Under normal conditions razorfish can be quite difficult to find, their presence often all but hidden beneath a rectangular slot in the sand. Many anglers become aware of a razorfish's presence only after a sudden spurt of water indicates that it has decided to make off, something that they can do with surprising speed. If you dig for them you will find that they are by no means the tractable beast that the lugworm is. Many a time I have had to dig furiously to catch one, usually when I have been digging for lugworm and come across a razorfish by accident.

An alternative method is to sprinkle salt in the holes. This brings the creature to the top, where it can be smartly seized. I have found this more effective if I first squirted a strong saline solution down the hole. (They are collected along the French coast with short, barbed spears for eating.)

Baiting

To bait with razorfish, run a sharp knife down the hinge. Open the shell and remove the white 'foot'. This can be threaded onto a hook or fished in the same way as fish strip.

Razorfish is best used immediately, or at least kept alive until needed. It does freeze but its flesh becomes softer after death, and extra caution is needed for casting. For distance casting a shop-bought device called a bait-pin will help. This consists of a piece of stainless wire twisted around the bend of a hook, laid beside the trace and secured by a tight plastic sleeve at the opposite end. However, home-made versions can easily be produced and are well worth the trouble to make. Not only is this arrangement ideal for razorfish, presenting the point clear of any impediment and supporting the bait during casting, but it is also useful with sprats and other soft baits such as a whole pouting mounted on conger tackle.

MUSSELS

In some areas these make excellent bait for flatfish. A big disadvantage is that their soft flesh makes them awkward and time-consuming to attach to the hook. This is partially compensated by the fact that they are so easy to collect. It is important that you keep them as fresh as possible, preferably gathering them immediately before the trip.

Baiting

To bait with mussel, which is very attractive to dabs and flounders, open the shell by inserting the tip of a knife just deep enough to sever the muscle that holds the shell together. Run the blade all the way round. Open the shell and scoop out the flesh with the knife, taking care to keep the creature as intact as possible. Take the point of your hook and pass it through several times, finally inserting it through the tough muscle.

This is not satisfactory for casting. You will need to tie the bait round with some elasticated thread to make it at all secure. Do this several times and tie it off, trimming the ends for neatness.

SLIPPER LIMPETS

These are found in colonies along the seashore, several attaching to larger limpets, and so they may be picked up in bunches. They are a variable bait, but this unpredictability is partly offset by the ease with which they may be collected.

To bait with limpets, scoop two or three from their shells and thread them on a hook, inserting the point through the tough part of the flesh. You will find that there are times, particularly after a storm has washed up hundreds on the beach, when fish become preoccupied with feeding on them. At such times your only chance of success depends on taking advantage of this situation.

CHOOSING BAITS

	EXCELLENT						GOOD						VARIABLE					
Bass	SR	PC	S	R			KR	L	P				HC	SQ	M	SL		
Mackerel	M	S					SQ											
Garfish	M	S					SQ											
Scad	M						S						SQ					
Pollack	P						SR	KR	SS	SQ	S		M					
Wrasse	SR	KR	P	PC	SS		HR	L	HC				R	MS	SL			
Cod	SR	L	PC	R			SQ						KR	P	HC	M	MS	SL
Whiting	SR	KR	L	P	PC	R	HR	SQ	M	S			SS	MS	SL			
Plaice	SR	KR	L	PC	R	MS							HR	SQ	M	S	SL	
Flounder	SR	KR	L	PC	R	MS							HR	P	SQ	SL		
Dab	SR	KR	L	PC	MS		R						HR	SQ	SL			
Gurnard	PC	SQ					M	S	R				KR	L	P			
Grey mullet	HR																	
Conger	M						SQ	S										

SR Silver ragworm   HR Harbour ragworm   KR King ragworm   L Lugworm   P Prawn
PC Peeler crab   HC Hermit crab   SS Sea slater   SQ Squid   M Mackerel   S Sandeel
R Razorfish   MS Mussel   SL Slipper limpet

CHAPTER FIVE

Knots

Every angler should know how to tie knots that are strong and do not come apart under pressure. Fortunately a few knots will suffice for every fishing situation.

The strongest knots are the Bimini hitch, blood knot and Palomar knot. Others that are helpful are the leader knot and the stand-off loop. It is also useful to know how to attach spade-end and plain-shanked hooks to nylon. The Bimini hitch I will describe in detail, but for instructions on tying the other knots see Figs. 23–26.

The Bimini hitch is exceptionally strong: no other knot can take as great a strain. It is also stiff and helps to prevent tangles. With care you can even tie little booms out of the trace itself. The stiffness of the knot, which could be as long as the angler chooses to make it, is very useful in a number of tackles.

If you are prepared to make a simple tool, you can tie Bimini hitches speedily and surely (Fig. 20). You will need a piece of ½ in (1.25 cm) diameter dowelling 3–5 in (7.5–13 cm) in length, Araldite and a wire coathanger. Pre-drill the dowel to accept the thickness of the wire, cut a piece from the coathanger and glue it in the dowel. Bend it as shown in the first diagram. If you put a slight twist in the wire at the stop, A, bending it back towards the main loop, you will find that a completed hitch slides off easily.

Once the tool is made you should check that the wire is seated securely in the dowel handle. If it is try making a Bimini hitch. At first the loops may not be as neat as you might like but they will steadily improve with practice.

Slip the line through the loop in the tool, making sure that the wire at A has line on both its left and right sides. Pull back on the tool with the left hand to make the line tight and hold approximately 14 in (36 cm) of spare line in the right. Keeping the line taut, begin to twist the tool, laying the line in the right hand neatly beside the main line.

As you twist the tool the lines wrap together. Allow this to a length of at least ½ in (1.25 cm) and stop. Turn the spare line towards the tool and continue to twist, guiding it so that it forms tight coils around the main line and back to the stop.

You are now ready to tie off. This is done by passing the spare line to the right of the stop, threading it through the loop of line held on the tool and back through the new loop that you will now have formed. Pull tight and repeat to the left of the stop and once more on the right. Trim the end but still keep the line tight.

Hold the main line up and release the tool. It will spin vigorously for a few moments as it gets rid of any twists in the line. Wet your thumb and forefinger, then draw them down the line to the tool. When all the visible twists have gone you can remove the knot by hooking it over the stop and sliding it off.

The important thing is to keep the line tight and not release the knot until the tool has stopped spinning. If you want to put a swivel on the loop then pass the line through it before passing the line — in the initial stages — to the right of the stop. It will then slide freely on the finished loop.

Attaching a plain-shanked hook to nylon
Some of the best patterns of hook available, such as the Partridge eyeless Aberdeen, cannot be attached

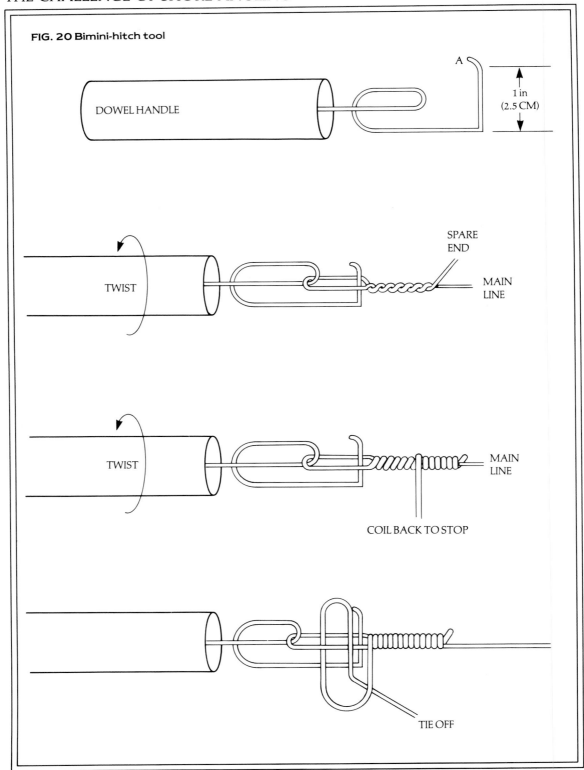

FIG. 20 Bimini-hitch tool

DOWEL HANDLE

A

1 in
(2.5 CM)

TWIST

SPARE
END

MAIN
LINE

TWIST

MAIN
LINE

COIL BACK TO STOP

TIE OFF

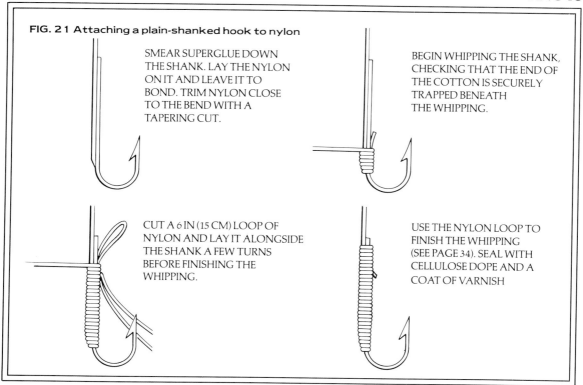

FIG. 21 Attaching a plain-shanked hook to nylon

SMEAR SUPERGLUE DOWN THE SHANK. LAY THE NYLON ON IT AND LEAVE IT TO BOND. TRIM NYLON CLOSE TO THE BEND WITH A TAPERING CUT.

BEGIN WHIPPING THE SHANK, CHECKING THAT THE END OF THE COTTON IS SECURELY TRAPPED BENEATH THE WHIPPING.

CUT A 6 IN (15 CM) LOOP OF NYLON AND LAY IT ALONGSIDE THE SHANK A FEW TURNS BEFORE FINISHING THE WHIPPING.

USE THE NYLON LOOP TO FINISH THE WHIPPING (SEE PAGE 34). SEAL WITH CELLULOSE DOPE AND A COAT OF VARNISH

to the line by conventional knots. However, the plain shank makes them ideal for worm baits, although superglue, cellulose dope and varnish are needed to attach them. To use these hooks properly it becomes necessary to tie the traces before going on a trip (Fig. 21).

Superglue is needed to bond the hook to the nylon, and the whipping is done with conventional thread. The dope shrinks the cotton for firm attachment while the varnish seals it. Eventually water will creep into the bond and dissolve the superglue, but until it does you will have a very secure hook. The best thing is to test each trace before you re-use them on a second trip.

Attaching a spade-end hook to nylon

With the exception of Breakaway and Partridge spade-ends there are few hooks of this pattern that I like. In the majority of cases a spade-end is a cheap hook, with a limited lifespan and still more restricted effectiveness. Many keen anglers avoid them altogether.

However, a spade-end damages baits less than an eyed hook and can be tied more quickly than a plain-shank. If you are tackling up at the beach a spade-end is useful for worm baits and, unlike a plain-shank, is ready for immediate use. Fig. 22 shows how to attach a spade-end to nylon.

Tying a spade-end hook by hand can take a lot of practice. It is fiddly but once tied the hook is very secure. However, MPH Associates have produced a tool they call the HUKTYA. This device is both ingenious and simple to use, enabling a spade-end to be tied in seconds. With practice it can also be used to make Bimini hitches. For those wishing to use spade-ends I would seriously suggest buying this tool — both for convenience and general strength. It is well worth the money and can also be used to tie hooks that have eyes.

Figs. 23–26 explain how to tie the other knots I have mentioned above.

FIG. 22 Attaching a spade-end hook to nylon

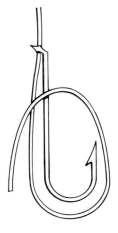

MAKE A LOOP ABOUT
6 IN (15 CM) IN DIAMETER
AND LAY IT BESIDE THE
SHANK.

TAKE THE END OF THE LOOP
NEAREST TO THE SPADE END
AND WHIP IT AROUND THE SHANK
AND DOUBLE STRANDS OF NYLON.

TUCK IT THROUGH THE LOOP,
PINCH THE COILS TO THE
SHANK AND PULL ON THE
SPARE END TO TIGHTEN.

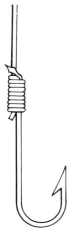

PULL ON THE TRACE TO FURTHER
TIGHTEN THE KNOT. SLIDE CLOSE
TO THE SPADE END AND PULL
FULLY TIGHT.

FIG. 23 Blood knot (a general-purpose knot)

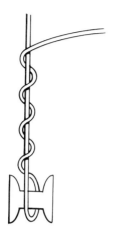

PUSH 5 IN (13 CM) OF LINE THROUGH
THE EYE. DOUBLE IT BACK AND TWIST
IT EIGHT TIMES AROUND THE
MAIN LINE.

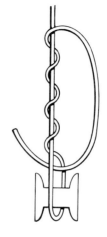

PUSH THE END OF THE LINE
THROUGH THE LOOP IMMEDIATELY
NEXT TO THE EYE (OF WHATEVER
IS BEING TIED).

TUCK THE END OF THE LINE
THROUGH THE LARGE LOOP
THAT WAS FORMED IN THE
PREVIOUS STEP.

PULL GENTLY ON THE LINE UNTIL
THE COILS FALL NEATLY INTO PLACE.
WET AND PULL TIGHT, AND TRIM
THE END.

FIG. 24 Palomar knot (a strong all-purpose knot)

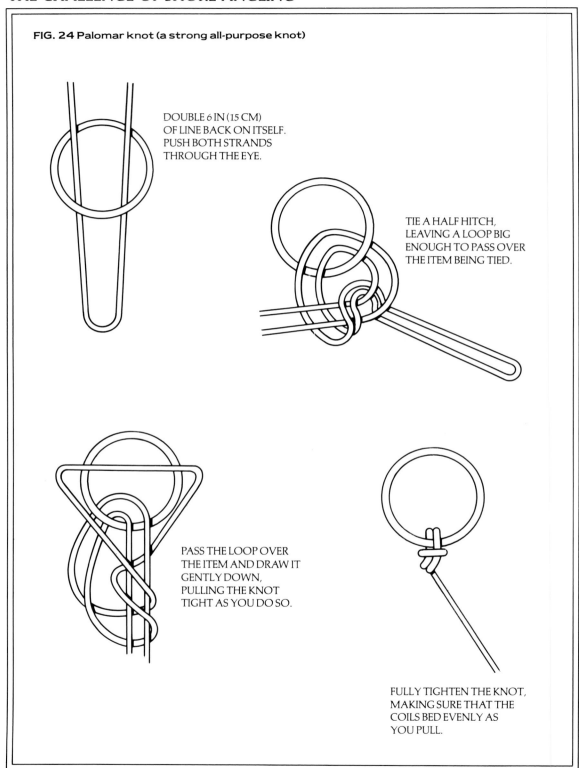

DOUBLE 6 IN (15 CM)
OF LINE BACK ON ITSELF.
PUSH BOTH STRANDS
THROUGH THE EYE.

TIE A HALF HITCH,
LEAVING A LOOP BIG
ENOUGH TO PASS OVER
THE ITEM BEING TIED.

PASS THE LOOP OVER
THE ITEM AND DRAW IT
GENTLY DOWN,
PULLING THE KNOT
TIGHT AS YOU DO SO.

FULLY TIGHTEN THE KNOT,
MAKING SURE THAT THE
COILS BED EVENLY AS
YOU PULL.

FIG. 25 Stand-off loop (a quick and easy way to make a paternoster)

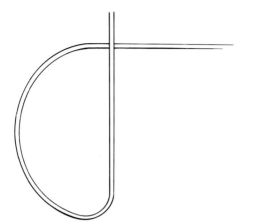

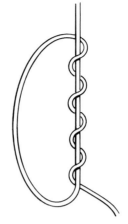

FORM A LOOP IN THE LINE
AT THE POINT WHERE YOU
WANT IT.

TWIST THE END OF THE
LINE THROUGH THE LOOP
SEVERAL TIMES. CHECK
THAT THE LOOP IS EXACTLY
WHERE YOU WANT. IF NOT,
AT THIS STAGE YOU CAN STILL
MANIPULATE IT UP OR DOWN.

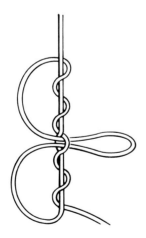

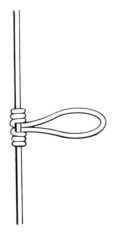

OPEN THE CENTRE OF THE
TWISTS AND PUSH THE MAIN
LOOP THROUGH IT.

LUBRICATE THE NYLON
AND PULL GENTLY TO
TIGHTEN UP. THE SUCCESS
OF THIS KNOT DEPENDS ON
THERE BEING SUFFICIENT
TWISTS. THE TRACE IS
ATTACHED TO THE LOOP.

FIG. 26 Leader knot (used to join two lines of different strength)

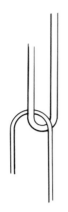

PLACE THE THICKER NYLON
AROUND THE MAIN LINE
AND DOUBLE IT BACK.

FORM A LOOP, COIL IT ROUND THE
MAIN LINE AND FORM ANOTHER LOOP.
TUCK THE END BACK THROUGH THE
FIRST LOOP FORMED.

PULL THE KNOT TIGHT AND TIE A
BLOOD KNOT WITH THE MAIN LINE.

TIGHTEN THE KNOT SLOWLY AND
WITH PLENTY OF LIBRICATION. TRIM
THE ENDS AS CLOSE AS POSSIBLE.

CHAPTER SIX

Mackerel and Garfish

The mackerel is a migratory species commonly caught on rod and line during the summer. They swim in midwater but will vary from this if chased by a predator, plunging to great depths in an effort to escape blue, thresher or porbeagle shark, their natural enemies. Mackerel will also descend to greater depths with the onset of winter.

As with any species, if we take the trouble to familiarize ourselves with the mackerel's lifestyle it should enable us to better understand and predict its movements. Mackerel hibernate during the winter, gathering in vast shoals that stay near the bottom. The main mackerel grounds are in the northern North Sea and the Skagerrak, between Denmark and Norway. It is also found in the waters to the south and west of the British Isles. It is thought, though not known for definite, that mackerel do not feed in winter. They are, however, both sluggish and particularly vulnerable, not so much to their natural enemies but to increasingly efficient commercial depredation.

In the spring the fish begin to rise to the surface, starting to feed once more but restricting themselves almost exclusively to a diet of plankton. This is sieved from the water entering the mouth by the gill filters. By April and May mackerel are present in coastal waters but are caught infrequently at that time of year. Spawning takes place between May and June off southern England, northern France and in the North Sea, while European stocks spawn in the eastern Skagerrak and the Kattegat, between Sweden and Denmark, during June and July. Spawning accomplished, the fish begin to feed very actively, breaking up into small shoals to chase herring, sprats and sandeels.

The mackerel is very easy to identify, most of us being familiar with it through its presence on the fishmonger's slab. The back is either blue or green, sometimes a mixture of both, with dark, wavy lines striping it in a random pattern. The flanks and belly are silver and the body is very streamlined. A spiny dorsal fin is situated just behind the head. Further back the adipose fin starts, just after the body begins to taper quite sharply. Between this and the tail are several miniature fins, almost like tufts. On the underside the anal fin begins a fraction forward of the adipose. The tail is very sharply pointed, like the head of a 'Y'.

The post-spawning active feeding period is when most anglers seek mackerel. A variety of methods are used successfully but a very popular one, which is also the least sporting, is the use of feathers. These are a multi-hook tackle that have dyed feathers whipped to each hook to imitate the sandeel. Feathers are normally worked in traces of three, four or six, and frequently produce what is termed a full house — a fish on every hook.

I have seen too many fish killed in this way just for the sake of it. Suffice it to say, the feathers are cast and allowed to sink. They are then pulled through the water as the rod tip is raised. The angler lowers the rod tip while reeling in until he is again in contact with the feathers. The process is repeated until the tackle is fully retrieved. Various speeds are used according to the circumstances. It's basically trial and error to discover the speed of retrieval that is most successful.

Feathers are useful for obtaining bait fish. They have nothing to do with sport or angling skill. Even so, some people find the method enjoyable.

A mackerel taken at one in the morning, while float-fishing for whiting

In the south and south-west of England, it is not unknown for mackerel to stay close inshore for longer periods than in other areas. Several years running they were caught from the shore in Torbay right up until Christmas. Unfortunately commercial pressure on the species has been so great as to cause a noticeable reduction in the level of sport. Over the last few years in particular mackerel numbers have dwindled rapidly. This is a great pity as it is a fast, hard-fighting fish that struggles gamely on appropriate tackle. It has no swim bladder and can dive to great depths without adverse effect.

A balanced approach is essential for obtaining the best sport. It is better to concentrate on the quality of the sport rather than the quantity. Some ultra-light tackle users enjoy first-class tussles on light, freshwater gear. But conditions are rarely so perfect as to allow the use of such tackle.

I like to use a light spinning or carp rod and a fixed-spool reel. The rings should be reasonably large and the whole outfit comfortable to hold.

Several nice combinations are available, a particularly impressive one being the DAM Magic Carbon Carp rod and the DAM CS40 reel, both of which have the advantage of being very reasonably priced.

However, for a superb fixed-spool at a very good price, the Shimano Magnum-Lite GTX 2200SS deserves serious consideration. For light tackle specialists it is going to be as close to their needs as anything else on the market, even being fitted with a lever drag that makes it a pleasure to use. For use with carp rods you'll need to step up a model, but with the prices much less than you might have imagined, this is a step that is well worth taking.

FLOAT-FISHING

A widely used method is the single-hook sliding float tackle (Fig. 27). This is used in conjunction with a long trace, normally baited with any of the following: mackerel or garfish strip, sandeels, pout,

An improvised tripod on Lannacombe beach

Mullet caught with Mepps spinner; both thick-lipped and thin-lipped mullet will hit baited spinners

ABOVE The twisted squint of the flounder, one of the most obliging of fish for the novice shore angler; abundant, attracted by almost any fish bait, and available all year round

BELOW Blenny feeding, ever watchful for predators, hugging the rocks

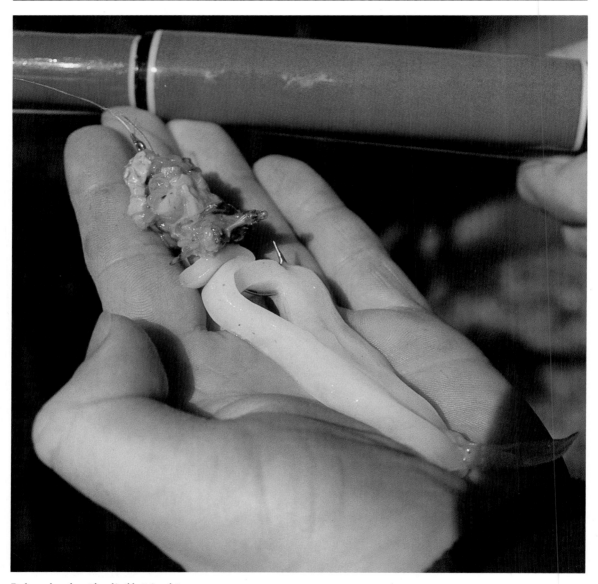

Peeler crab and squid cocktail bait for plaice

Rock fishing amidst the grandeur and solitude of the north Cornish coast

The greatest prize: bass, taken at night on the flood tide

Mick Brown shows a conger caught on light tackle; wherever there are rocks, there is a good chance of finding conger, especially if the rocks lie close to the entrance of a harbour

For anglers like Charles Armstrong, access is the major problem; flat concrete surfaces are ideal. When fishing from convenient breakwaters or piers, it is almost always necessary to winch the fish up vertically or drag it over ground, so a heavier line than usual is recommended.

FIG. 27 Single-hook sliding float tackle

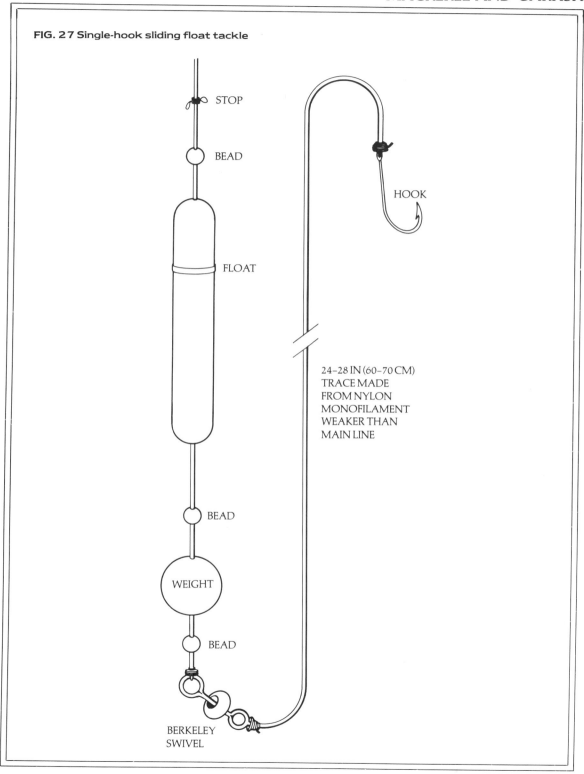

STOP

BEAD

FLOAT

HOOK

24–28 IN (60–70 CM)
TRACE MADE
FROM NYLON
MONOFILAMENT
WEAKER THAN
MAIN LINE

BEAD

WEIGHT

BEAD

BERKELEY
SWIVEL

squid or cuttlefish strip, rockling, tiny eels, whitebait and sprats.

Live sandeels and livebait in general all serve to catch larger specimens than are usually taken on strip bait. One of the most selective is a 4–5 in (10–13 cm) pout. It is hooked once only, through the upper jaw, and cast a little distance. Sometimes it may be taken by a bass, but I am sure you will not be too disappointed if it is!

When you use float tackle, the depth at which the float is set to work could be anything from 6 ft (1.8 m) to over 40 ft (12 m) in depth. A good starting point might be 14 ft (4.5 m) in clear conditions, fishing shallower or deeper until the mackerel are found. Generally, if the day is warm, go shallow, if cold, deeper.

A mackerel bite is indicated by the float shooting underwater. It must be struck at once as any delay will usually result in the fish getting away. If you do miss the bite just leave the tackle alone for a couple of minutes and give it a couple of twitches. This will often induce another take. If not, reel in very slowly, stopping every 10–12 ft (3–3.5 m) and allowing the float to settle. Sometimes mackerel will follow with the retrieve and attack again.

An adaptation I favour for roving competitions is float tackle with two hooks (Fig. 28). I still enjoy good sport with mackerel but often catch a garfish at the same time. In fact, if you set the tackle at a shallow level you may even find it difficult not to catch two garfish at once. This is a very useful tactic for building up a good match weight.

The booms shown in the diagram can be either home-made or tied out of the traces themselves. The latter is done with Bimini hitches, the line being placed about the stop but not threaded through the loop on the tool.

A 2 in (5 cm) hitch is then tied, the nylon being stretched at the end to accommodate the finishing knots. A tiny loop is then revealed through which you must place the line and complete the hitch in the usual way. Slide off the hitch after letting the tool spin, and then thread your main line through the loop end of the hitch. Tie a dropper loop at the appropriate point but, instead of pushing through the central opening with the main loop, use it to catch the first ¼ in (0.5 cm) of the hitch.

For single-hook tackle I normally use line of 8 lb (3.5 Kg) b.s., but with two hooks it is best to increase this to 12 lb (5.5 Kg). I do this not only because of the possibility of catching two fish at once, but also because I might want to increase the size of both the weight and the float, so that I can cast further.

Do not get into the habit of using a float solely for daytime fishing. On page 26 you will find instructions for making an electric float that you can see clearly at night. Experiment and you will find that mackerel can often be caught right through the night, although if they go deep you can be plagued with small whiting.

SPINNING

Another effective method for catching mackerel is spinning. Use the lightest rod possible and match this with small, flashy spinners on around 6 lb (2.5 Kg) b.s. line. When you catch a fish on this gear the fight can be very good indeed. As spinners you can use krills, tobies, westenders, small plugs or red gills. A useful lure is the white 65 mm (2¼ in) red gill.

If the spinner is heavy enough to cast without weight use it without. Cast it and vary the speed at which you retrieve the line, to simulate the darting movements of a small fish. Sometimes it is effective to just drop the rod tip, in the middle of retrieving the line, and allow the lure to flutter downwards for a second or two like a stricken fish. Reel in again and often a fish will take.

For soft-bodied lures, which need extra weight for casting, it is best to simply reel in at varying speeds, perhaps with an occasional movement of the rod tip to give an added incentive to a curious fish. Slide a ball weight on your line, then a bead, and tie on a swivel. To the other eye of the swivel tie a 4 ft (1.25 m) trace and attach the lure. If you like you can increase the length of the trace — the aim is simply that the lure should not follow too closely behind the weight.

Garfish

When fishing for mackerel you will often encounter the garfish. This travels around the shore in much the same way, and is sometimes found in such close proximity that it has earned the local

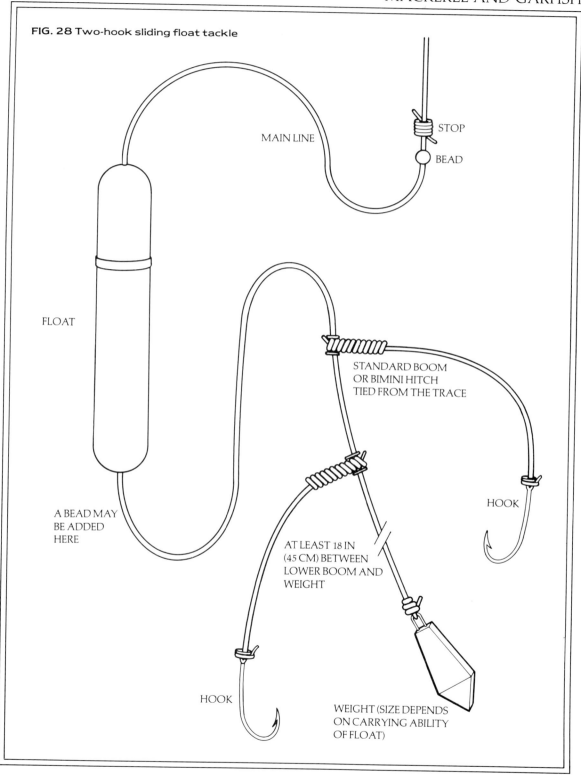

FIG. 28 Two-hook sliding float tackle

MAIN LINE

STOP

BEAD

FLOAT

STANDARD BOOM
OR BIMINI HITCH
TIED FROM THE TRACE

HOOK

A BEAD MAY
BE ADDED
HERE

AT LEAST 18 IN
(45 CM) BETWEEN
LOWER BOOM AND
WEIGHT

HOOK

WEIGHT (SIZE DEPENDS
ON CARRYING ABILITY
OF FLOAT)

Float-fishing for garfish at Hope's Nose in Torbay

names of mackerel-guard and mackerel-guide. It is shaped rather like a giant sandeel, but with a different arrangement of fins and long, pointed jaws lined with sharp teeth. The back is blue-green and the flanks and belly are silvery-white. The scales are rather small but the epidermis, a thin and almost transparent outer layer, is composed of larger, quite brittle segments.

Garfish can often be caught when sport with mackerel is flagging, enlivening the action with their leaps and determined dives. They also seem to be indifferent to members of the shoal disappearing from their midst, so the level of sport remains steady.

For children taking up fishing, garfish can provide both enjoyment and the incentive to continue. However, I would suggest that you return any unwanted garfish to the water as soon as possible. On the one occasion that I used a keepnet they poked their beaks through the mesh, so I let them go to stop them hurting themselves.

Another time a shoal stayed on the feed for several hours, keeping to a small area. They were in the company of mackerel, neither fish showing a preference for a particular bait, although mackerel strip was the most used before I arrived.

To achieve the best catch, I had drop-netted a good supply of tiny pout from a harbour wall at 4.00 am. These were kept alive with an aerator until I arrived at my mark. Then they were attached to single-hook float tackle and cast into the shoal. Over the next four hours I took 26 garfish, 11 mackerel and two pollack.

Given the same bait, conditions and tactics, anyone could have done the same. I worked out the state of the tide before I selected which spot to fish, gave up a few hours' sleep to make sure that I had good bait and then used a proven method.

The problem of deep hooking

On several occasions I have landed deep-hooked garfish, which often give little or no indication that they have been hooked until it is too late. To try to stop this happening I experimented with various floats until I came up with a combination that worked. I adapted a West Country float (Fig. 29). I used a countersink on the top of the float and made

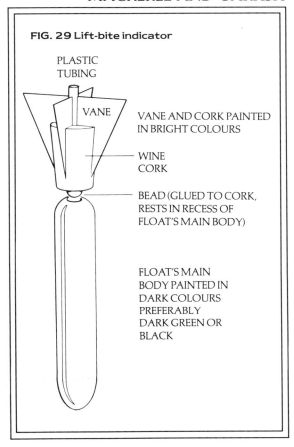

FIG. 29 Lift-bite indicator

PLASTIC TUBING

VANE

VANE AND CORK PAINTED IN BRIGHT COLOURS

WINE CORK

BEAD (GLUED TO CORK, RESTS IN RECESS OF FLOAT'S MAIN BODY)

FLOAT'S MAIN BODY PAINTED IN DARK COLOURS PREFERABLY DARK GREEN OR BLACK

a small recess. Then I drilled a wine cork lengthwise and used the countersink on the narrowest end, making a small hole. Into this I glued a bead, making sure that the hole in the bead lined up with the hole in the cork. I glued a plastic tube into the hole in the cork, made an incision and inserted a plastic vane. Two coats of paint sealed both float and indicator.

When I tested this device, in which the line passes through the indicator and the float, I found that the weight pulled the top down and settled the bead into the recess in the top of the float. A stop to trap the weight against the swivel was also helpful. If a garfish tried a lift-bite the indicator fell on its side long before the main body of the float, giving me ample warning to strike. The problem of deep-hooked garfish was solved.

Garfish are not usually so capricious. They usually take in a rapid manner that leaves their intentions in no doubt. However, on very hot, settled summer days it is useful to have such a device in case they become lazy and behave unpredictably.

Like mackerel, garfish can also be caught by spinning. However, I find that the best lure is simply a strip of mackerel flesh hooked once and trailed at least 4 ft (1.25 m) behind a ball weight. Alternatively you can use a small, flashy spinner, with the emphasis on 'small'.

If you intend to take either mackerel or garfish for eating, be discriminating about the size of the fish that you keep. A minimum size that would allow the fish a chance to breed at least once would be 12 in (30 cm) for mackerel and 16 in (40 cm) for garfish. The latter, despite their odd appearance, make excellent eating. I admit that I was a bit squeamish at first, particularly when I discovered they had bright-green bones, but I was pleasantly surprised. The flesh is both firm and dry — in fact, very tasty.

As for the green bones, which is incidentally another nickname for the species, they are nothing to worry about. The colour comes from an entirely harmless pigment.

A fair-sized gar; contrary to all appearances, excellent eating!

CHAPTER SEVEN

Pollack

The pollack, sometimes called the lythe, is a sporting fish caught mainly from Britain's southern coasts. It is a close relative of the coalfish and a member of the cod family. In appearance it is very similar to the coalfish and this often causes confusion. To distinguish between the two species look at the jaws and the lateral line. In the coalfish the lateral line is straight and the jaws roughly level. The pollack has a protruding lower jaw and a lateral line that curves over the pectoral fin (the fin on the side, just behind the head).

The pollack has a green-bronze back, which lightens down the flanks. The coloration then takes on a yellowish tinge frequently flecked with gold. The body is streamlined but designed for sudden rushes rather than sustained high speed. When first caught the pollack is a handsome fish, but its looks disappear after death. Then the colours fade and the flesh begins to deteriorate, so much so that after 24 hours, unless frozen, it is unwise to risk eating it.

The overall shape of the pollack suggests a predator that ambushes its prey. The protruding lower jaw helps it to seize its quarry from beneath. The body reinforces the impression, being more suited to dashing in for the kill than to chasing for prolonged periods.

What does this tell us as anglers? Simply that if pollack like to ambush their prey, then we should look for them where they have plenty of cover. Most often this will be where weed-covered rocks offer plenty of hiding places from which pollack may attack. Here they might browse through the weed, keeping a watchful eye both in front of and above themselves. The prey appears in the target

Anthony holds a coalfish taken from a moored yacht. Harbours often contain large shoals of either these or pollack

range and the pollack dashes from cover, seizes it and dives for cover again.

When you catch a pollack you will find that the first rush of the fish is the strongest dive of the fight. If the fish is a big one let it have its head for a moment and yield line. Once the first rush is over

The large eye and predatory jaws of the pollack

you will be able to control the fight better. If the fish does not feel too big keep a tight line (bearing in mind its breaking strain) and force the fish to exert considerable effort to take line from the reel.

FLOAT-FISHING

If you live in an area where nearly all of the fish caught are fairly small try using coarse-fishing tackle for maximum sport. As for the floats, forget ultra-light quills — simply buy a sliding pencil float in the smallest size. This will balance with a weight of about ¼ oz (7 gm) and can be set up in the same way as the sliding float rig shown on page 51.

When you get a fish on this tackle — using line of no more than 6 lb (2.5 Kg) b.s. — you will have to play the fish carefully. Most of them will not be over 2 lb (1 Kg), but at least you will get good sport with them.

You will often find hordes of smaller pollack in harbours, and they also turn up, though not in the

same numbers, around piers on an otherwise sandy beach. If you try fishing from a pier don't cast too far, because the fish will usually be hiding underneath the pier itself.

If you were to travel northwards, eventually you would find the pollack in harbours being replaced with shoals of coalfish. Both species can be fished for in the same way so don't worry about using lots of different methods. Stick to a few reliable ones such as float tackle, spinning with rubber eels and legering with an added buoyancy device.

Although this book is primarily concerned with shore fishing, I would advise anyone who gets the chance to fish for pollack or coalfish from a boat moored inside a harbour. The sport can be very rewarding, even though the boat may only be tied up to the harbour wall.

To return to float-fishing, there is something about a float disappearing underwater that sets the adrenalin flowing. For children it is an ideal method and also one that many women enjoy. Most float-fishing is done during the day, but for pollack the most productive period is dusk and full night. I have already described a home-made electric float (see page 26) and another alternative is to use a Starlite attached to a conventional float. Basically this is a small plastic tube filled with chemicals. When a Starlite is bent and shaken the chemicals mix and a reaction begins that generates light for up to ten hours.

To attach the Starlite to the float I use some rigid plastic tubing the same diameter as the Starlite (Fig.30). I cut off a piece about 1 ½ in (4 cm) long and whip and superglue it to the plastic core protruding beyond the end of a West Country float. I then cut a piece of silicon rubber tubing, making sure that it is a tight fit, and place one end over the rigid plastic while the other secures the Starlite.

When float-fishing for pollack, don't try to cast over the horizon! At night, particularly from rocky marks, they come close in. A 20 ft (6 m) cast is usually enough to put you among fish, especially if you fish beneath where a light shines onto the water. Sometimes, when fishing just such a spot, I have not bothered to cast but have simply lowered a prawn into the water. No tackle except for a hook, and I have still enjoyed good sport.

SPINNING

Spinning is also used to deadly effect, lures such as red gills, westenders and Eddystone eels accounting for large catches. Other successful lures are tobies, German sprats and krills. Whichever lure you use, try to work it as close to the bottom as you can. Nice and slow is the way, with sudden spurts before allowing the lure (if it is an eel) to flutter gently back. For spoon-type lures such as tobies never stop reeling in. If you miss a take either speed up for a few moments or slow down.

When you spin for pollack you must accept that loss of tackle will be inevitable, for weed and rocks in combination take many spinners. Also watch the direction in which you cast, as a sideways spin with 90 per cent of the cast over rocks has more chance than a straight cast where 50 per cent of the distance might be over sand. You will have to judge for yourself at the time. If you cast straight and know

that it is rocks all the way in, well and good. If part of the distance is over sand adjust your tactics accordingly. Remember also that to work the lure near the bottom you must give it time to sink once it hits the water. If using a fixed-spool leave the bail arm open until it stops taking line. If using a multiplier you will notice a slight jar when the weight touches bottom.

LEGERING

As for leger tackle, set it up as in Fig. 31. The buoyancy device is simply a drilled, miniature float set between two stops. The trace should be long, at least 4 ft (1.25 m), preferably 6 ft (1.8 m) and the float should be between one third and two thirds of the length of the trace from the hook. The nearer to the hook it is set, the higher the hook will ride off the bottom (which is the purpose of the tackle) and the bait will be in plain sight of fish skulking near the bottom. If there are pollack about, the bait will be slightly above them — an ideal attack position which will often trigger bites.

Distance casting is usually unwise as the fish are more often than not under your feet. Also, pay attention to the weight that you use for casting. Why waste money on leads — even home-made ones — when a stone with a hole in it, picked off the beach and costing nothing, will give you all the distance you need?

For more exotic fishing, if you have fly-fishing equipment try using it with a large, white feathery lure worked on a sinking fly line. Often this will catch pollack — particularly in harbours with large shoals — and the fight is most entertaining.

Whichever method is used, take care when unhooking and returning any unwanted fish. Throwing them into the water from even a few feet will stun the fish and make them vulnerable either to seagulls or drowning. (A fish takes in water through the mouth, over the gill-rakers, where oxygen is extracted, and passed out of the gills. If the gills are flooded from behind while the fish is weakened, it may not have the strength to expel the water and breathe properly.)

Above all when fishing for pollack, remember that they are opportunistic predators; consider the size of the eyes and you will realize that they are

FIG. 30 Attachment of a starlite to a float

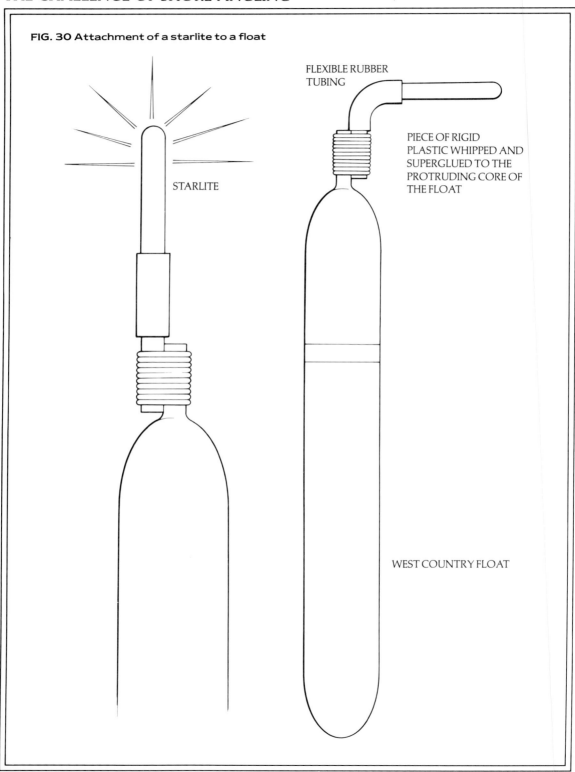

STARLITE

FLEXIBLE RUBBER
TUBING

PIECE OF RIGID
PLASTIC WHIPPED AND
SUPERGLUED TO THE
PROTRUDING CORE OF
THE FLOAT

WEST COUNTRY FLOAT

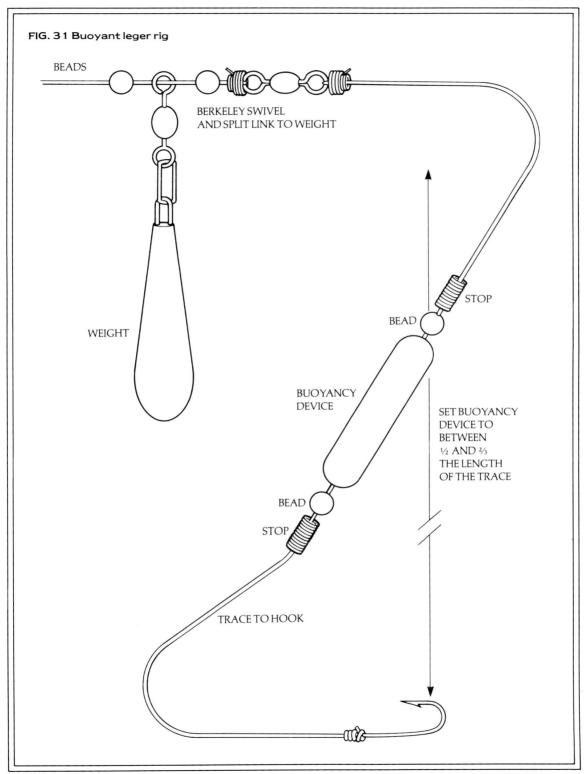

FIG. 31 Buoyant leger rig

BEADS

BERKELEY SWIVEL
AND SPLIT LINK TO WEIGHT

WEIGHT

STOP

BEAD

BUOYANCY
DEVICE

SET BUOYANCY
DEVICE TO
BETWEEN
½ AND ⅔
THE LENGTH
OF THE TRACE

BEAD

STOP

TRACE TO HOOK

attracted primarily by visual stimuli. When spinning, try to give life-like movement to your lure. Sometimes pollack will shoot up through a shoal of fish taking as many as possible before diving down again, so don't fish too high in the water in the daytime, or your bait will be ignored. Pollack rise in the water as dusk approaches. Be prepared to move from one rock ledge to another in search of the fish, bearing in mind that pollack tend to stay in wait for

unwary passing quarry in one place, rather than moving about actively seeking a meal.

As for eating, if pollack are fresh they are delicious, but after 24 hours forget it. If you intend to keep them in a freezer for consumption later simply gut the fish, wrap it in cling film and put it straight in the freezer. Try to keep the flesh as dry as possible — though obviously it will be repeatedly immersed during gutting — as this will help it to stay firm and tasty.

CHAPTER EIGHT

Flatfish

More than a dozen species of flatfish are found in British waters, belonging to three main families — turbot, plaice and sole. There is a wide range of sizes, with tiddlers that only grow to a few inches long to the massive halibut weighing hundreds of pounds.

The turbot family includes the turbot, brill, topknot, Bloch's topknot, Norwegian topknot, megrim and scaldfish. Apart from turbot, brill and megrim, the rest are small fish, not really of interest to the angler. Your chances of connecting with a megrim are very remote as it lives in deep water of 25–220 fathoms (45–400 m). They are occasionally caught by boat anglers, but few shore marks offer such a depth of water.

Turbot and brill grow to a large size, with turbot in excess of 30 lb (14 Kg) recorded from both boat and shore. The brill does not reach such an impressive size but it does attain weights of well over 10 lb (4.5 Kg). To distinguish the two apart you need only look at the back. In the turbot there are tubercules on the upper side but no scales, whereas the brill has scales but no tubercules. Generally, the brill also has a more southerly distribution than the turbot, which is found all around Britain's coasts.

Both species are determined fish eaters, making a meal of such creatures as sandeels, whiting, pout, dragonets, pilchards and other small fish. They show little or no interest in worm baits, which may account for the relatively small numbers landed by anglers.

TURBOT
To fish specifically for turbot, stick to a fish bait, with perhaps a crustacean in reserve. Most anglers connect with either turbot or brill when they are fishing for bass, usually with a small to medium livebait. Fillets of fish have also taken their share of turbot over the years. Sometimes peelers catch, but not very often.

On one trip I fished the lower jetty on Bournemouth Pier, where I have seen turbot taken on occasion. I set up a sliding float tackle slightly over-depth so that the float was resting on its side while the weight was on the bottom.

Currents run along the shore, not towards it, so when the tackle had settled in the water it was caught by the current and drifted away from the pier. With the weight dragging along the bottom and lifting on every swell, the effect was that the bait, on a 4 ft (1.25 m) trace, was following behind the little disturbances when the weight kicked up sand as it touched the bottom.

Small flatfish are usually curious about such disturbances as they often indicate the presence of a likely meal. I figured that what worked for small flatfish might well work for large ones. The bait was a sandeel on a 2/0 fine wire hook. It was only recently dead so I used a hypodermic syringe to inflate the stomach so that the eel would be more visible to the fish.

On the two occasions that I tried this tactic I caught three small turbot — each about 2½ lb (1 Kg), returning them as they would not yet have had much chance to breed. As far as sexual maturity is concerned, the male matures faster than the female, but any turbot less than 19 in (50 cm) is unlikely to be mature.

Since that trial I have experimented with various tackles and baits and have come to the conclusion

Plaice taken with a spoon and coloured beads

that leger tackle is probably the best bet, but that the trace should not be less than 5 ft (1.5 m) long. This makes casting a bit of a problem, so I devised a small refinement that makes it much easier (Fig. 32). I took a second hook, with a turned-down eye, filed off the barb and secured it to the trace 2 in (5 cm) over the bait, using telephone wire to secure it in position. A variation on this set-up is to include a buoyancy device to lift the bait higher in the water. Alternatively, you can inflate the bait with a hypodermic needle.

When I cast I simply hung the barbless hook over one of the wires on the Breakaway. This held it during the cast but fell off when it hit the water, provided of course that the hook was upside down as shown. I gradually came to look upon both sandeels and sprats as the best baits, although it is difficult to get hold of really fresh sprats. You may also have to use a bait-pin to hold them during casting.

It is worth trying for turbot. They are not a common fish but they are more prevalent than many people think. Persevere and your efforts will probably be rewarded, if not with turbot then possibly with bass, conger or rays.

PLAICE

Species in the plaice family are more often caught by anglers, plaice, dabs and flounders all being regularly taken on rod and line. Other members of the family include the lemon sole, witch, long rough dab, halibut and Greenland halibut.

Although flatfish spend most of their lives searching for food on the seabed, they do not hatch as small flatfish but as tiny, round fish. When they first appear they have one eye on each side of the head and look much the same as the young of many other species.

For a short while these tiny fish swim in the upper layers of the sea, but then their lives begin to change and they head for the bottom, where they begin a remarkable transformation. Here they lie on one

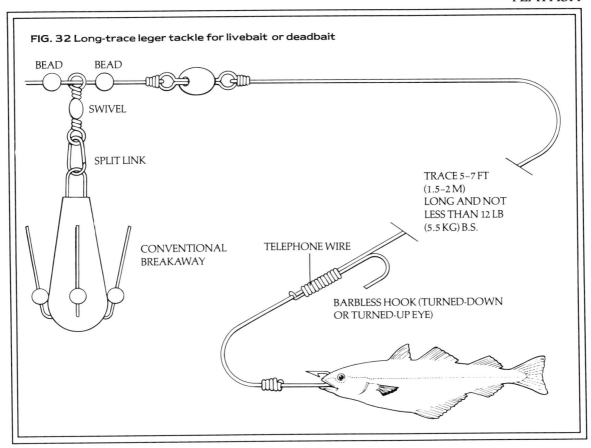

FIG. 32 Long-trace leger tackle for livebait or deadbait

BEAD   BEAD

SWIVEL

SPLIT LINK

CONVENTIONAL
BREAKAWAY

TELEPHONE WIRE

TRACE 5–7 FT
(1.5–2 M)
LONG AND NOT
LESS THAN 12 LB
(5.5 KG) B.S.

BARBLESS HOOK (TURNED-DOWN
OR TURNED-UP EYE)

side of their body, which starts to assume the flatness of their adult form. At the same time the eye on the blind side begins to migrate across the head until both eyes are close together and facing upwards.

The body coloration assumes two contrasting shades. The upper side turns brown and takes on a camouflage pattern that matches its environment while the lower turns white. In the flounder the underside may be blotched with brown and the white rather murky. This is particularly prominent when they are found in estuaries or just after leaving them for the open sea.

Identification
Plaice, flounders and dabs resemble each other very closely, leading often to mistaken identity. The surest way to distinguish them apart is by touch. If you stroke the fish from tail to head, each will feel different. The dab's skin feels rough, and while the flounder's is smooth there is a row of bony tubercules down the lateral line and along the base of the fins. If the fish is a plaice the skin is smooth and these tubercules are absent. The plaice may have orange spots, sometimes ringed, but these may also turn up on big dabs, although the rings will not be present.

Plaice and dabs favour different haunts to flounders, although occasionally they are all present at the same time. Plaice are usually found over sandy bottoms, sometimes fine gravel, while flounders prefer a muddy bottom, being found in large numbers in estuaries and natural inland harbours such as Poole.

If you ever eat a beach-caught flounder, you will find that it tastes much better than its estuarine relations. Plaice and dabs are also very tasty, particularly if cooked within a few hours of capture.

A good-sized dab taken on legered carp tackle

A broad guide for minimum size would be to return any dabs under 9 in (23 cm) in length and any plaice or flounders under 12 in (30 cm).

METHODS

The most popular methods of fishing for flatfish are various types of leger or paternoster tackle. Float tackle can also be successful from places where it makes sense to use it.

Standard beach tackle is often employed, if not usually needed. Many anglers equate flatfish with distance and consequently aim to hurl their tackle out as far as possible. Sometimes they do well, particularly from beaches where the gradient is very shallow, but often they cast well beyond the distance that they actually need. Even if they are successful, there is little sport in dragging in a plaice that is completely outgunned by the tackle. The angler simply winds it in like a dog on a lead.

Far more sporting is to use leger or paternoster on carp rods and reels. A good caster can still hit 100 yards (90 m) — if he needs it — but when he connects with a fish, it can often put up a spirited struggle. Fairly often a cast of 60 yards (55 m) is all that is required to put your bait among fish, and sometimes even less.

I am not suggesting that every angler would be better getting rid of beachcasting tackle and using carp gear — just that sometimes it can be a lot of fun to use. Whether or not it is practical for you depends on where you fish. For example, the tide race in Weston-super-Mare makes a nonsense of using such an outfit, similarly the masses of weed off Dungeness make it completely unsuitable. In other areas a carp outfit is ideal, doubling up as a very effective float and spinning rod.

One of my favourite marks is where a rocky headland eventually gives way to sand. It attracts large flatfish, but you need a good cast to clear the rocks and masses of snags that are closer in.

Anthony Nockolds and a small-eyed ray

Beachcasting tackle enables you to do this — and the rewards are often worth the effort. From this particular spot I have taken dabs to 1 lb 11¼ oz (0.8 Kg), plaice to 3½ lb (1.5 Kg) and flounders to 2½ lb (1 Kg). Trawlers cannot get too close, because of the risk to their nets, and so the fishing is surprisingly good. Nearly every area has such a spot, so find yours.

SPOON FISHING

Another method for flatfish is the baited spoon. The most popular pattern was the 10 gm (⅓ oz) ABU Rauto, but unfortunately this went out of production. The good news is that very effective copies have since appeared.

The spoon is a lure which trails a baited hook. The wobbling motion attracts the flatfish closer, and when they arrive they find the bait, usually lug, rag or peeler crab. It can be a killing method, but it is more successful from a dinghy than it is from the shore.

The most important consideration is that the spoon should be worked with the current, not against it. From a beach this might mean casting out, walking 100 yds (90 m) along the beach, letting out line as you go, and then retrieving the tackle, slowly and appetizingly. However, if there are several people fishing, such an approach will not make you any friends. More sensible locations are the sides of piers and also bridges over or near the mouths of estuaries. Harbour walls are also well worth investigating.

Make sure that the hook is fairly close behind the spoon, certainly no more than 6 in (15 cm). (I try for 2 in (5 cm) behind the furthest point of the blade.) Don't be afraid to experiment, but takes will definitely lessen the farther away the hook is. Try different sizes of spoons. I have caught gurnard and wrasse on a 4 in (10 cm) spoon, but have taken plenty of eels on a much smaller lure.

Spoons can also be used as attractors on conventional tackle. Not the heavy kind but light, small plastic teaspoons with the handle removed. These are drilled at one end and threaded onto a split ring which in turn is connected to a swivel. The eye of the swivel runs along the trace and the spoon is free to revolve about the line. Spoons of this kind

are particularly effective for flounders, but you do need a few spares as the plastic eventually breaks and falls off.

When I use these spoons as attractors, I usually thread a stop onto the trace, followed by a bead, the other eye of the swivel and another bead. Then I tie on the hook. The stop is secured about 6 in (15 cm) from the hook (Fig. 33). This serves the double purpose of securing the spoon in the vicinity of the hook and ensuring that worm baits are not pushed up the trace by the air resistance encountered during the cast. Attached in this way the spoon wobbles well, setting up a distinct series of vibrations in the water.

Although disposable teaspoons are usually made out of white plastic, they are sometimes available in red. If you can get hold of these, it is often worthwhile having a few made up ready in the tackle box. The reason for this is that on a day with bright, sunny conditions the normal white spoons may flash and scare off any fish that might otherwise be interested. The red spoons don't suffer from this problem as they don't have the same reflective properties.

Coloured beads are also used as attractors, an effective combination above the hook being red — orange — red — orange — red. Green is not so effective and white is variable; blue is useless.

From time to time you will encounter problems with crabs, particularly in estuaries, where they may reach plague proportions. On a bad day they will strip your bait within a couple of minutes of it hitting the bottom. The only effective answer is to use a buoyancy device. This should cure the problem, except on the rare occasions when you find that your mark has been invaded by swimming crabs!

TACKLE

As far as tackle is concerned, I like to use a paternoster for estuaries and beaches and a leger for casting over rocks (not into, which is an entirely different situation — see rotten-bottom tackle on page 83) and from piers. Generally, the paternoster is for longer-distance work, but the leger will deal with bigger fish more efficiently. Which you use is entirely up to you.

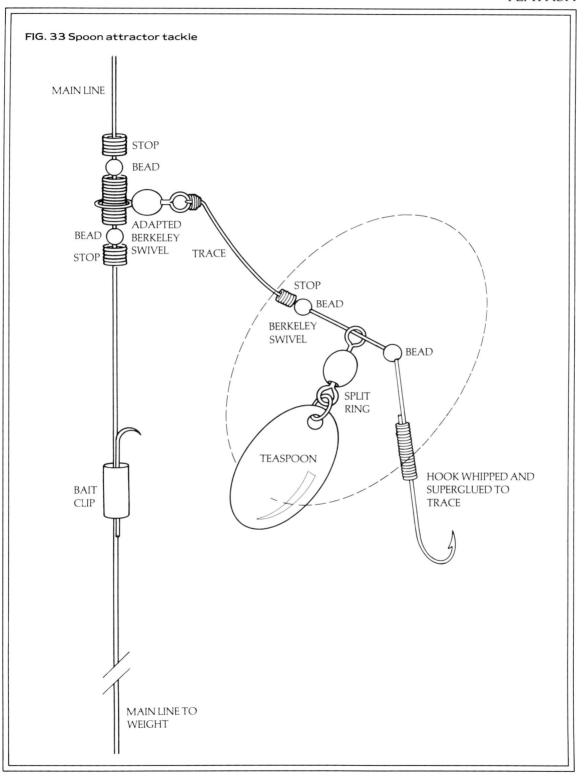

FIG. 33 Spoon attractor tackle

MAIN LINE

STOP

BEAD

BEAD

ADAPTED
BERKELEY
SWIVEL

STOP

TRACE

STOP

BEAD

BERKELEY
SWIVEL

BEAD

SPLIT
RING

TEASPOON

HOOK WHIPPED AND
SUPERGLUED TO
TRACE

BAIT
CLIP

MAIN LINE TO
WEIGHT

While plaice and flounders respond vigorously to a bait used with a buoyancy aid, with or without a spoon, I have rarely caught dabs in this way. When I have caught them, they have only been small. Once I caught two of only a few ounces, removed the buoyancy aid and caught three of over 1 lb (0.5 Kg) on successive casts. Nor is this an isolated incident, but something that has happened again and again. I suspect that the smaller fish, less cautious perhaps than their older relatives, are much more active during the feeding period, the lure of the food off the bottom overcoming their natural inclination to stay hidden in the sand, or at least to be able to bury themselves in seconds.

When I am after the bigger dabs, I usually fish with a running leger, but never use a trace more than 18 in (45 cm) long. My favourite bait for such trips is silver ragworm tipped with the claw of a peeler. As an added incentive I often let two legs trail on the bend of the hook, hooked lightly through once.

Seasonal factors

The time of year plays a big part in determining the size of catches of flatfish. Flounders are resident in British waters for most of the year, but fishing for them peaks between November and January, just before they spawn. At this time the adult fish will travel down and out of estuaries and harbours, heading for spawning grounds in the open sea. Beach anglers positioned along their migration path will frequently enjoy an exceptional and rewarding level of sport. Dabs are also present for most of the year, but will usually absent themselves for a short time between January and March. The biggest dabs are usually caught in the autumn.

Plaice are caught throughout the summer and well into autumn and winter, but are in poor condition during the spring when they have only just returned from spawning.

Other plaice

Returning to the rest of the plaice family, the lemon sole is not a true sole but a flatfish reminiscent of the dab. However, it can be distinguished from its cousin by its smooth skin. There are also patterns of variegated colour on the back, which is basically brown, but which displays a marbled effect of yellow, green or orange. It is a fish rarely caught by shore anglers, although its distribution actually is widespread. An angler wishing to catch one would be wise to scale his hook down to size 8 and fish with worm baits.

The long rough dab is found around the northern half of Britain's coasts and may even be abundant in some areas. It is a small fish that generally does not exceed 12 in (30 cm) in length and 9 oz (0.25 Kg) in weight.

On the other hand, although the witch grows to a larger size, specimens up to 19 in (50 cm) having been recorded commercially, it is a deep-water species that does not come sufficiently close inshore for anglers to meet it in any great numbers. It is fairly abundant in the Irish Sea, but before you leap aboard the ferry I should perhaps point out that it favours soft ground at depths of 35–50 fathoms (65–90 m).

Halibut and Soles

The halibuts are the biggest of the flatfish tribe, growing to over 400 lb (180 Kg) and can usually be recognized by their size or their green backs. They prefer to live at depths of over 50 fathoms (90 m), so they are ruled out for the shore angler.

The soles number among their ranks the sole, (known as the Dover sole) sand sole, solenette and thick-back sole. Of these the sand sole is very rare, the solenette attains a length of 5 in (13 cm) and the thick-back sole is only slightly bigger with a maximum length of 9 in (23 cm).

The sole is the only member of the family worthy of the angler's efforts. Besides being very tasty, it can reach 24 in (60 cm) in length and weigh over 4 lb (1.8 Kg). Its distribution is mainly southerly, but it nonetheless covers a wide range and is plentiful in many areas.

Although not taken on rod and line as frequently as anglers might wish, there are certain times when sole feed more vigorously than usual. For example, although the sole is a nocturnal feeder, if you are fishing during the period when the sun starts to come up, you will often find that the bites come thick and fast for a short but hectic time.

On one occasion a friend and I had seven sole in

half an hour. We had scaled our hooks down to a size 8 with ragworm bait, but found that sport started and stopped in a very sudden manner. One minute we had not had a bite for ages — the next we were catching.

Further trials seemed to indicate that this period was indeed something special for sole, and also demonstrated that the same principle applies when darkness finally settles after a gathering dusk. Certainly, you need not be up before dawn to catch them — you can always give up a few hours' sleep at the other end of the night.

CHAPTER NINE

Wrasse

Seven species of wrasse can be found in British waters, though there are also many tropical species. Those native to our coasts are the ballan, rainbow, corkwing, cuckoo, scale-eyed, rock cook and goldsinny. Of these only the ballan and cuckoo wrasse are worth fishing for, the others being too small. You will probably encounter rainbows from time to time, these being voracious little fish, but by far the majority of the wrasse taken by anglers are ballan wrasse, which grow to a large enough size to be interesting.

Cuckoo wrasse will occasionally turn up, these growing to a length of about 14 in (36 cm), but the ballans are much bigger fish, with specimen ratings of 5 lb (2.25 Kg) in some areas. Wrasse are, however, purely a sport fish and not worth trying to eat.

The ballan is a stocky, fairly long fish with a powerful build and well-muscled jaws capable of pulling limpets from the rocks. The teeth are very strong and there is a second set in the throat. The scales are large, while the fins have a reddish tinge that can be marked with white spots. Coloration is usually green and brown, although males often have a more handsome livery than the females, particularly when they are small.

The usual diet of both species of wrasse consists of barnacles, tubeworms, crabs and molluscs, but they will take with enthusiasm a range of baits, including ragworm, peeler crab, prawns, lugworm, sea slaters, razorfish and clams. Occasionally they take sandeel strip, and on more than one occasion I have caught large specimens while legering with live sandeel.

For novice anglers wrasse are often a good introduction to the sport. They are easy to catch, both on float or leger tackle, and they fight hard enough to keep the interest from flagging. They are also convenient in that they can be caught throughout the day (but not at night), accept a wide range of baits, and can be kept in a keep net for periods without suffering harm. They also make excellent subjects for an angler wishing to chart his progress with photographs.

Wrasse become lethargic as night falls, preferring to lurk in rocky lairs rather than rooting through the weeds in search of something to eat. Many divers have been fascinated by the sight of them resting on their fins and apparently asleep, and have reported how they can usually be found like this right through the night, only beginning to stir after the sun has been up for a while. I have often wondered whether this has anything to do with temperature, for wrasse, like other fish, have a metabolism that is accelerated or slowed by the temperature of their surroundings. As it gets warmer, so the food they consume is processed more rapidly, forcing them to eat larger quantities. When the temperature drops their metabolism slows down and they do not need to eat as much as they did.

This process can be seen clearly during the summer. A trip to some rocky mark, invariably the haunt of big wrasse, will result in hectic sport. A return to the same mark in the winter will produce a fraction of the bites, and perhaps one or two decent-sized fish. This is why it pays to use a big bait during spells of colder weather. The fish are still there, but they are lethargic, even torpid. They are more likely to take one large piece of food than root round for lots of snacks. This is, after all, more energy-conserving, a survival tactic for a period

A reasonable ballan

when the food supply is in short demand.

Winter sport can be very patchy, depending on where you fish. Basically, the lower the water temperature drops, the more irregular the fishing will become. So if you fish in the South, around Plymouth or Torbay, for example, you can expect to catch wrasse almost right through the winter. The further north you go, the less are the chances of this, especially as wrasse are very susceptible to the more severe changes in the temperature. During a particularly cold spell in 1963 there were a considerable number of fatalities, from which the stocks took several years to recover.

There are several methods available to the wrasse angler, the most popular being leger, the 'rotten-bottom' paternoster and float-fishing. All of these tackles have been tried and tested for several years, but with the addition of a few simple pieces of home-made terminal tackle they can be both improved and made cheaper.

'ROTTEN-BOTTOM' TACKLE

Fig. 34 shows 'rotten-bottom' tackle. You will notice that the weight has been replaced with a sparking plug. This is a trick that will also work with leger tackle. All it requires is the manufacture of a simple, stainless wire clip as shown in the inset. A piece of silicon rubber slides over both the clip and the top of the sparking plug, the line sliding freely through the eye at the bottom of the clip.

The biggest wrasse are usually to be found in the most snaggy areas of rock. Tackle losses are inevitable — and can be expensive. If you replace weights with sparking plugs picked up from scrapyards for a few pence each, you will at least save money on weights.

The other inset shows a second style of clip, again made from stainless wire but with an optional two swivels secured to the eye. The main line is tied to one swivel and a length of weaker trace, perhaps as light as 6 lb (2.75 Kg) b.s., is tied to the other, the

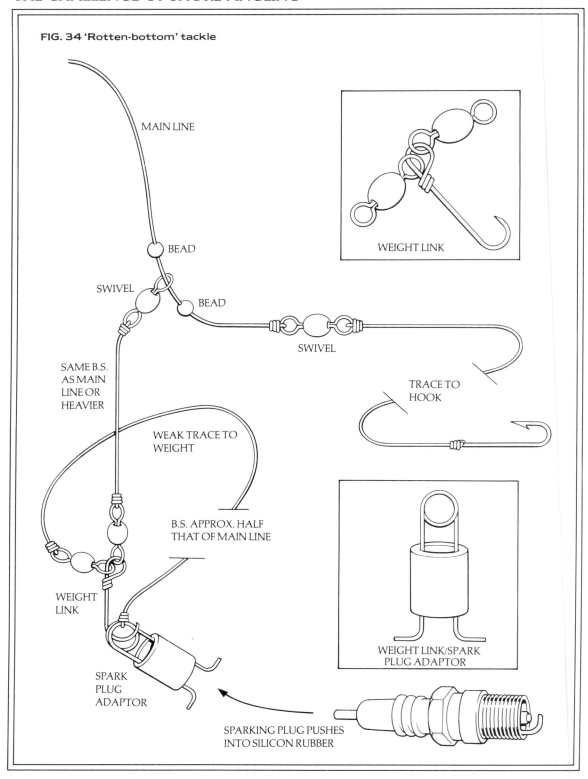

FIG. 34 'Rotten-bottom' tackle

MAIN LINE

BEAD

SWIVEL

BEAD

SWIVEL

WEIGHT LINK

TRACE TO HOOK

SAME B.S.
AS MAIN
LINE OR
HEAVIER

WEAK TRACE TO
WEIGHT

B.S. APPROX. HALF
THAT OF MAIN LINE

WEIGHT
LINK

WEIGHT LINK/SPARK
PLUG ADAPTOR

SPARK
PLUG
ADAPTOR

SPARKING PLUG PUSHES
INTO SILICON RUBBER

weight being attached to the other end. For casting, the weight is hooked over the clip. When the tackle hits the water, the lead falls off and is secured to the line by the weaker length of trace. If it gets snagged the trace will break and you can still recover any fish that you have caught, along with the main body of your terminal tackle. The swivels are optional, as you can tie the main line and the weaker trace directly to the eye of the clip.

FLOAT-FISHING

Float tackle is most effective through the summer. If baited with sea slaters, ragworm, peeler or prawns, it will usually draw wrasse in large numbers. However, you may find that sport comes in little flurries, perhaps with the most fun at the top of the tide. If it is a little patchy be as mobile as possible, as sometimes a walk of only a few yards will put you back among the action.

There are some marks where the water floods up over rocks that have a low covering of weed. These may be landfalls or even man-made tips of rocks that have yet to acquire a healthy covering of kelp or a similar growth. Such habitats attract small animals, such as sea slaters or shrimps, in large quantities, but they usually dry out when the tide ebbs. Wrasse will appear with the rising tide, hunting for food with a ferocity perhaps prompted by the limited time available for their search.

Some of these wrasse are very large, but they can be fished for with lighter tackle than normal. Float-fishing is very effective, as is free-lining (the only tackle being the baited hook tied to the line) with prawns and peeler or soft-backed crabs. A light spinning rod delivers the bait with the hook set to ride either on or just off the bottom.

A wrasse hooked in such an area gives a fight that is very different from that of one hooked in deeper water. Cover is, after all, minimal, and the fish make long runs and determined dives in an effort to reach it. Over the years I have hooked several that have come up and swirled on the surface, dived and swirled again, all in an effort to throw the hook. They seem to really come alive, fighting with an abandon that I have not seen matched by their brethren, hooked in more conventional localities.

You can try freshwater tackle in spots such as this,

The author about to unhook a 2 ½-lb wrasse caught on leger tackle

but I would not fancy your chances against a fish of 5 or 6 lb (2.25 or 2.75 Kg). I have tried it, even landing a few of the smaller ones, but I did not have much luck against the bigger fish. Better to stick to rods with a bit more power.

For most large wrasse beachcasters or even boat rods are used. This approach often works, but it can completely outgun the majority of the fish being caught. I prefer to use a 2 ½ lb (1 Kg) test-curve carp rod, matching it with a light multiplier such as an ABU 6500. The rod has the length to put leverage

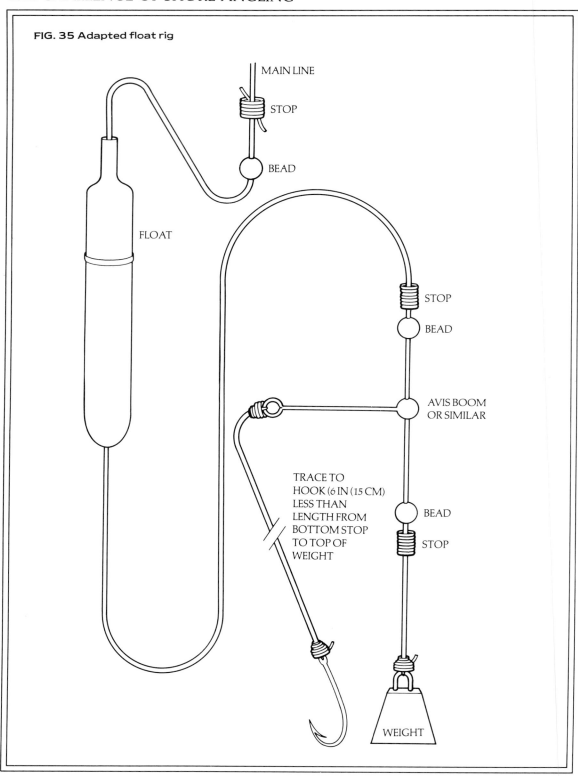

FIG. 35 Adapted float rig

MAIN LINE

STOP

BEAD

FLOAT

STOP

BEAD

AVIS BOOM
OR SIMILAR

TRACE TO
HOOK (6 IN (15 CM)
LESS THAN
LENGTH FROM
BOTTOM STOP
TO TOP OF
WEIGHT

BEAD

STOP

WEIGHT

on the fish, steering them away from cover, while the reel has the sensitivity to deal with any sudden dashes. The reel's disadvantage is its rate of retrieve. A fixed-spool is much faster but lacks the finesse of the drag system on a multiplier.

One of the main problems of wrasse angling is their teeth. These can bite through quite thick monofilament. The problem can be countered in several ways — for example by scaling down to 6 lb (2.75 Kg) b.s. trace, using dental floss, scaling up to a 30–40 lb (14–18 Kg) b.s. trace or even using nylon-covered wire.

Adapted floating
Another tackle for large wrasse is an adapted float rig (Fig. 35). A big ballan can be very wary of float-fished baits, perhaps playing with them for a while before deciding to take them in earnest. To help them make up their minds I changed from conventional float tackle to a rig which presented the hook, on a short trace, just off the bottom. The trace was attached to a free-sliding boom on the main line, set between two stops a few inches apart. If a wrasse played with the bait the boom allowed the hook sufficient movement to allay its immediate suspicions. By the time the fish realized the danger I had usually set the hook.

Other advantages of this tackle are that it keeps the hook away from the weed, giving the angler a slightly better chance of not getting snagged. On normal float tackle the hook runs below the weight, and is often swept by the current into the nearest clump of kelp. If a wrasse takes in this position its chances of getting away are clearly improved. It is, after all, already sitting in the midst of cover. But with the hook above the weight the fish is not quite so near to safety.

Once you have caught a wrasse you should simply unhook it, admire it quickly and return it to the water. They are useless for eating and the flesh may even be harmful, tainted by the impurities that are being continually pumped into the water through our shameful and archaic sewerage systems.

It is not a good idea to put lots of wrasse into a rockpool, even if you intend to put them back later. The oxygen in the water is quickly exhausted and the fish may die. The temperature of the water may also rise far above that of the sea. When you do return the fish the shock of the colder water may do them severe damage. Far better to take a quick photograph, or use a keepnet, suspended in the sea, to store the catch and take a picture just before you release the fish carefully.

CHAPTER TEN

Bass

The capture of a decent bass is a red-letter day in the diary of most sea anglers, as it is probably the most popular fish found in British coastal waters. It grows to a large size, fights well and makes excellent eating. Unfortunately, it is also one of the species most vulnerable to commercial depredation, resulting in its current scarcity and controversy over what restrictions should be placed on nursery areas.

There is no doubt that the bass needs protection — at the least the imposition of a size limit of 18 in (45 cm) for both pleasure and commercial fishing. It also needs guarding against gill nets, overfishing and the destruction of its natural habitats. As anglers we must also play our part, not bending the rules hypocritically but observing meticulously the strictures that we would impose on others to protect the species.

No one should deny the angler the pleasure of eating a bass, but to fish simply for profit is something else. Bass fetch a high price, and doing the rounds of the hotels with the product of an evening's bass fishing can turn a handsome profit.

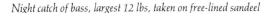

Night catch of bass, largest 12 lbs, taken on free-lined sandeel

Indeed, some anglers fish for bass in the hope of doing just that. We have no right to stop them doing so, but we can try to discourage them, pointing out that the breeding potential of a large bass is much higher than that of a young fish. It is a matter of simple logic: a large bass will lay far more eggs than a small one, and consequently the chances are that more will survive to maturity. If we return more fish to the water, more will survive to breed another year, so improving both the chances of the species and, in turn, the quality of our sport.

HABITATS AND HABITS

The bass is a handsome fish with a metallic-blue back, silver sides and a white belly. The body is covered in rough scales and there are two separate and quite distinct dorsal fins. The first of these is endowed with sharp spines, of which the angler should be wary, taking care also to avoid those on the gill covers.

Bass usually migrate into our inshore waters during the period from March to May. In some areas they never move far away from the shore, and so can be caught right through the year. They travel in shoals and forage widely for their food, some entering estuaries as far as fresh water, others hunting along the coastline amongst rocks, along beaches and inside and around piers and harbours.

Shore fishing often peaks in June and continues through July, after which large numbers of bass move further offshore for the richer pickings. They are still easily accessible to boat anglers, but the shore angler must choose his mark carefully, often finding a second rush occurs in September, with odd fish appearing until November or even later.

During the summer bass tend to pick their hunting grounds with sufficient regularity to give them the appearance of being territorial. For example, at the top of the tide they might appear at one reef for a couple of hours and then disappear to return with the night tide. In the meantime they may be feeding at another shore mark, or may have moved out of casting range in pursuit of a shoal of baitfish. Alternatively, they might forage around a headland, going one way with the tide and then returning when it changes.

You will discover your own bass marks as your experience grows. Most anglers keep theirs a jealously guarded secret, fearing, perhaps rightly, that otherwise hordes of anglers will descend on their mark, or, far worse, that it will be gill-netted and the stocks removed. There is no simple answer — the only thing to do is to look for likely marks, fish them at various stages of the tide (the top two hours often being the most productive, especially when they coincide with early morning or late night), record your results and keep them to yourself. Gradually you will acquire a series of marks, and it is a good idea to fish these lightly rather than exhaust the sport after two or three days of consecutive visits.

So what makes a likely spot? Bass can be taken from a variety of habitats, some sandy, some rocky, some completely artificial such as the inside of harbours. The answer is the food supply. At the mouths of estuaries, for example, there are usually sand bars which are rich with sandeels. Bass take advantage of the proliferation of food, several shoals sometimes meeting to feed actively for a period that may last for several hours. Rocky headlands are often inhabited by swarms of pout, and if the shoals move on the bass will probably follow. Beaches are good either during or just after a storm, when the seabed is disturbed and rich with easy pickings. Piers and harbours are often rich sources of fish offal thrown into the sea by charter boats and anglers.

It may also be that bass become pre-occupied with particular food species. During a storm, with the beach littered with razorfish and clams, they may ignore everything else, or be very finicky about what they take. Similarly, at headlands, if the water abounds with small pout try those for bait, as the chances are that they are what the bass will be feeding on. During June and July, when the rocky marks will be full of peeling crabs, bass may accept nothing else. To find out for yourself, you have to do your homework on your own local marks.

Bass will always make the most of what opportunities the sea may offer. If they encounter a shoal of baitfish then they will usually turn and pursue them, feeding actively until such time as their attention is diverted. Often the presence of seagulls, wheeling and diving over the water, will

Sea trout may appear on spinning tackle

give away the position of bass chasing fry from underneath. If a storm produces a glut of clams, bass will not turn their nose up at the chance of a free snack. Similarly with anglers' baits. Often the most popular marks fail to produce a bass during the day. At night, with far less people about, shoals of bass may forage closer, feeding on bait thrown into the water or on injured or dying fish returned earlier in the day. The best tactic here is to increase the size of whatever bait you use, preferably presenting a whole fish bait either on or just off the bottom.

Freelining is often a good method in these circumstances, especially with a small livebait such as a live sandeel or pout. Don't worry about not being able to cast very far as bass sometimes come much closer than many anglers imagine. I have seen good catches of bass taken from spots as little as 20 ft (6 m) from the water's edge.

Legering also works, but keep the tackle as light as possible. There is little need for heavy weights, except perhaps on a surf beach, and when fishing inside a harbour you can scale right down to a ½ oz (15 gm) or even less, for preference using a non-toxic lead substitute.

FLOAT-FISHING
Also effective is float-fishing, particularly in shallow water with a self-weighted float. These floats incorporate a weight in the polystyrene or plastic main body. When a fish investigates the bait there is no weight in the vicinity of the hook, and so less to arouse its suspicions.

Be careful about the size of float that you use. The bass — or indeed any species of fish — has got to pull the float underwater for the bite to register. Obviously resistance will be caused by the natural buoyancy of the materials from which the float is made. The smaller and slimmer the float, the less this resistance will be, and similarly the weight required to cock the float will be lighter. If you use a large float, the quicker the bass will reject the bait, reducing your chances of connecting. Alternatively try using the smallest, slimmest pencil float you can find, for preference at night with a Starlite adaptor such as that described on page 69. This rig offers little resistance to a taking fish, encouraging positive takes and aiding hooking.

SPINNING
Another successful method for bass is spinning. The tackle can either be unweighted — for example, large metal spinners (not so good) or plugs (very good); or weighted — an artificial eel, say, following in the wake of a small bullet. Also effective is a combination of both. If you substitute a metal spinner for a weight, replacing the treble hook with a swivel, you can tie a rubber eel to a short trace in the immediate wake of the spinner. Suitable lures for this purpose are Cebars or German sprats (Fig. 36).

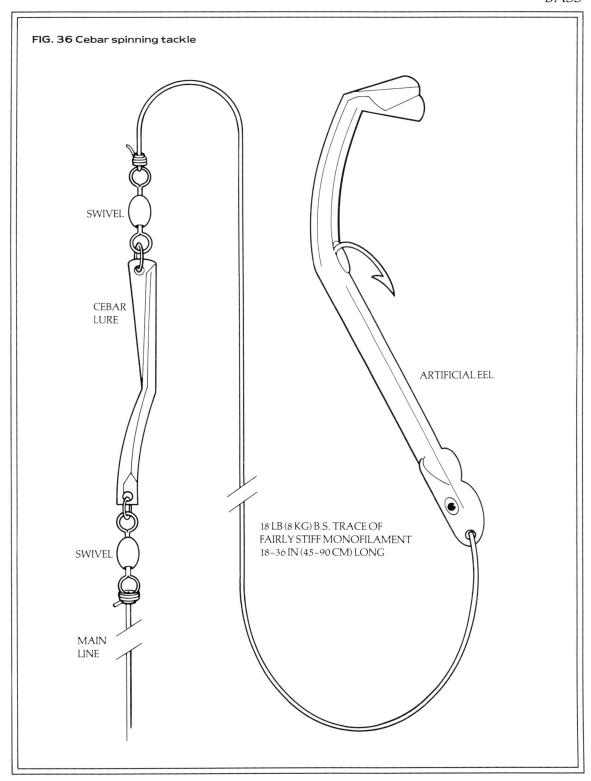

FIG. 36 Cebar spinning tackle

SWIVEL

CEBAR
LURE

SWIVEL

MAIN
LINE

18 LB (8 KG) B.S. TRACE OF
FAIRLY STIFF MONOFILAMENT
18–36 IN (45–90 CM) LONG

ARTIFICIAL EEL

When I have tested this tackle, it has definitely shown an advantage over fishing either type of lure on its own. What I suspect happens is that the first lure attracts the fish's attention, while the second triggers the decision to feed. Another factor is that the movement of the spinner adds to the movement of the rubber eel, generating a semi-circular movement that makes the lure react in a similar manner to a stricken eel.

Whatever the reasons for this tackle's success, you will find it effective for many species. By substituting flies for the eel, admittedly in different patterns, I have taken herring, scad, mackerel, pollack and gurnard. Also, varying the speed of retrieve will help to target particular species. A slow wind-in brings the lure near the bottom. The faster you go the closer it planes to the surface. Bass go for the slower speeds, as do pollack and gurnard, while the other species tend to like the faster movement.

DEADBAITING

Spinning with a mounted deadbait calls for preparation. If you plan to add metal vanes, such as those removed by chopping up a mackerel spinner, you really need to have several ready at the beginning of the evening's fishing so that you can change your bait quickly after a bass has ripped your offering to shreds. Or you can fish really simply, just hooking a small fish in the usual way, casting it out and retrieving it very slowly, tickling it over the tops of the weed.

The mounted deadbait rig that I use comprises a 4 ft (1.25 m) trace with a hook tied at both ends (fig. 37). I double the trace back at the halfway point, slide on a stop, a small bead, a metal vane from a mackerel spinner, a bead and two more stops, both of them as small as possible. The first stop I secure 4–6 in (10–15 cm) from the hooks, depending on the size of bait being used. The second secures the beads and mackerel vane immediately above the first. The final stop goes ½ in (1.25 cm) from the end of the loop formed in the line. This helps to keep the tackle tidy, the trace being attached to the main line via a swivel and link.

To mount the bait I pass each hook through the gills, one to each side of the body, then turn the hook and pass it through the fish just before the tail.

In this way both hooks lie in a straight line but face in opposite directions. The stops are slid down the trace to just before the head. A final touch is to tie the mouth shut, ensuring a nice planing action through the water.

A variation of the tackle described above is to pass the hook through the flesh several times, so that the fish hangs as straight as possible. Suitable baits for this tackle are sprats or pout, although you can adapt it to take other species such as atherines or blennies, although the last are the least effective bait that I know. There is no need to use weights with this tackle, as the deadbait has enough casting weight on its own. If you add weight to the main line, you will not improve the action of the bait but you will be increasing the likelihood of putting the fish off.

When this tackle works properly it can be very effective. However, I have often found problems if there are a number of mackerel in the area, as they usually take the bait before anything else has a chance to do so. This can be very annoying but is sometimes very good fun, especially if the mackerel are larger than usual. On occasion I have also taken small turbot on this tackle, usually from piers during daylight, recovering the bait slowly over a sandy bottom. When sprats come into harbours in September, it can be deadly.

FLY FISHING

Another method for bass, assuming you have got the equipment already or are prepared to buy it, is fly fishing. This can be very successful over the sand bars at the mouths of estuaries, and can also work in other locations. However, the majority of the time it is a method of taking 'schoolies', the smaller bass, but not a tactic for specimen fish (at least not in my experience). The Cebar tackle shows more potential with larger flies as it enables you to cover a wider area of water.

Fly fishing can be fun, affording entertainment not only with bass but with coalfish, pollack and herring. However, I would ask you to take care with the size of fish that you end up taking home. The method does catch a lot of small fish. Put them back to fight another day, hopefully when they are a bit bigger and wiser.

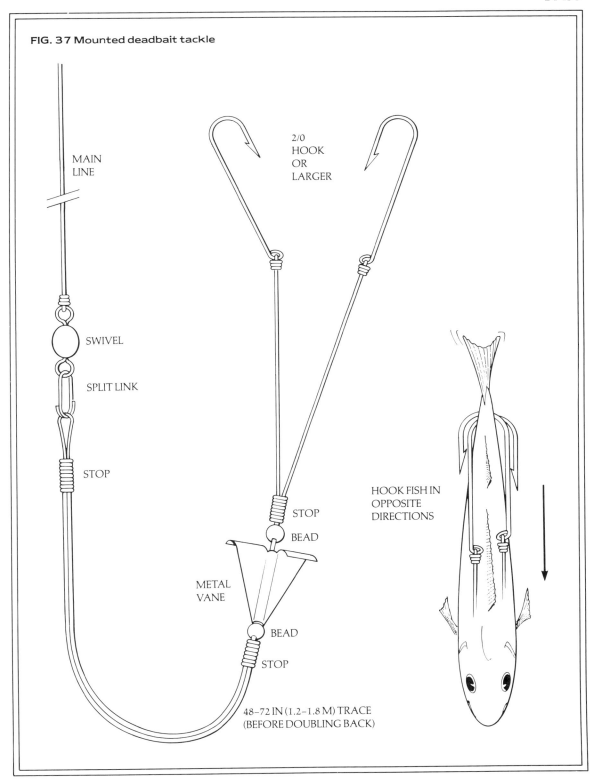

FIG. 37 Mounted deadbait tackle

MAIN
LINE

2/0
HOOK
OR
LARGER

SWIVEL

SPLIT LINK

STOP

STOP

BEAD

HOOK FISH IN
OPPOSITE
DIRECTIONS

METAL
VANE

BEAD

STOP

48–72 IN (1.2–1.8 M) TRACE
(BEFORE DOUBLING BACK)

Devon angler, Andy Fletcher, and a 10-lb bass

LEGERING

I have already mentioned that bass feed both during and immediately after a storm, when it pays to fish a sandy beach, for preference with the baits with which the beach will be littered. You will also find that legering is the only effective method during the storm itself. A spiked lead will hold the bottom securely, while a plain sinker will be washed ashore fairly quickly, covering a great deal of ground in the process. Which you use is up to you, but a spiked lead, cast just behind the third breaker from the shore, should eventually find fish. These may include not only bass but the occasional flounder and other flatfish that have come inshore for the same reason.

Don't use electronic alarms during the storm as they will sound all the time owing to the breakers plucking at the line. Use them from headlands when it is reasonably still — no more than Force Four. Here they will be effective, as they will be from piers and breakwaters.

I have covered a variety of methods in this chapter, and perhaps given you food for thought, but if you want to catch large bass then you will need patience, perseverance and luck. There are things you can do to boost your chances, such as adding a swimfeeder to paternoster tackle when fishing from a beach or headland, situating it just above the weight and securing it in position with a bead and stop. Plug the swimfeeder full of cotton wool and soak the wool in some pilchard oil or a scent attractor such as Biotrak — on which I reserve judgement, my own tests being inconclusive — resulting in a scent trail being laid up near your bait, with luck persuading bass to come closer and find your hook. Other things can be quite simple — using big baits, for example.

Whatever you do, don't fish with the drag on your reel set too tight for the fish to take line from the reel. A big bass will usually run, and you will want it to take line under pressure to tire it — not snap your line because the drag was too tight.

Another thing to remember is to be very careful about noise. Bass can be very shy when they are feeding, and a car starting next to the water, perhaps from a slipway, can startle the shoal and scare them away. A similar result is produced when headlights suddenly flash on the water's surface or excessive movement is highlighted by a light behind. The presence of swimmers will curtail sport straightaway, although the bass may return some time later.

Try to avoid noise wherever possible, and if you want to talk then do it quietly, as sound travels over water and it can give you away. Leave your radio at home. Be careful of your own movement, and remember that a wall or a cliff behind you will make your movements very difficult to distinguish from the water. A streetlight will have the opposite effect.

The bass is a fine fighter and a worthwhile adversary. Given time and motivation, you will eventually take a big fish. If you do then I would suggest that a photograph is the best way of keeping the memory alive as it lets the fish live as well. If it is the only bass of the night, then fine, keep it for food; but if you have caught some smaller ones let them go. In time it will reward us all.

CHAPTER ELEVEN

Grey Mullet

Three types of grey mullet are found in British waters — the thick-lipped, the thin-lipped and the golden grey mullet. The thick-lipped is by far the most commonly caught, although areas such as Christchurch in Dorset have large stocks of thin-lips. It is the thick-lipped variety which grows to the largest size, specimens of over 10 lb (4.5 Kg) having been recorded on very rare occasions. All three species are streamlined in appearance, with fairly large scales. They have two dorsal fins that are spaced well apart.

The thick-lipped grey mullet can be identified — surprise — by the thickness of the upper lip, which is much greater than that of the other two species. It is almost equal to the radius of the eye.

The golden grey and thin-lipped can be told apart by both coloration and the height reached by the pectoral fin. In the golden grey mullet this rises vertically to just beneath the first dorsal, whereas the pectoral of the thin-lip does not reach nearly so far. The golden grey mullet also has a golden tint on its flanks and golden spots on its head, characteristics lacking in the other species.

Golden grey mullet are rarely landed by anglers, while increasing numbers of the other species are taken every year. All three are surrounded by a body of angling folklore, which claims that they are intelligent, almost impossible to catch, and so on. The fact is that most mullet can be caught, provided that your approach, bait and tackle are perfect, or at least nearly so. It is vital that you assess each fishing situation correctly, paying close attention to the depth, food available, cover and any other factors such as water noise or boat traffic, before deciding on a particular way to fish. If your formula is right

you will catch mullet. If not, can you stand being frustrated for hours, days, even weeks by a fish of apparently highly discerning appetite and manner?

You think I am joking, but I once met a chap who tried for five weeks, afternoon after afternoon, to catch a member of a shoal that was fairly resident in an estuary. He tried small ragworm and bread paste, maggots and cheese, mackerel flesh and liver, mussels and tripe, all to no avail, until one day he brought some shrimp sandwiches with him for lunch. The mullet were as always clearly visible, swimming round and round his bait with total nonchalance — until he put on a shrimp from his sandwich.

Now bearing in mind that a shrimp that has been boiled, soaked in brine and tinned is hardly natural fodder, the mullet responded to this offering with an enthusiasm that took him by surprise. After his initial amazement he went on to catch half a dozen with the remains of his sandwich.

Surely, you say to yourself, he went back the very next day to the same spot, armed with tin upon tin of potted shrimps, and made one of the largest catches of mullet ever. He did go back the next day . . . and the next . . . and the next . . . until he caught a small flounder that just snuck up on his tackle. But no more mullet — not that season anyway.

The moral is this: on that one day he caught fish by being in the right spot, at the right time, with the right bait. However, the chances are that not far away there was another shoal of mullet. It would have been better, on the days when he persistently

Mike Bailey and a catch of Brixham mullet

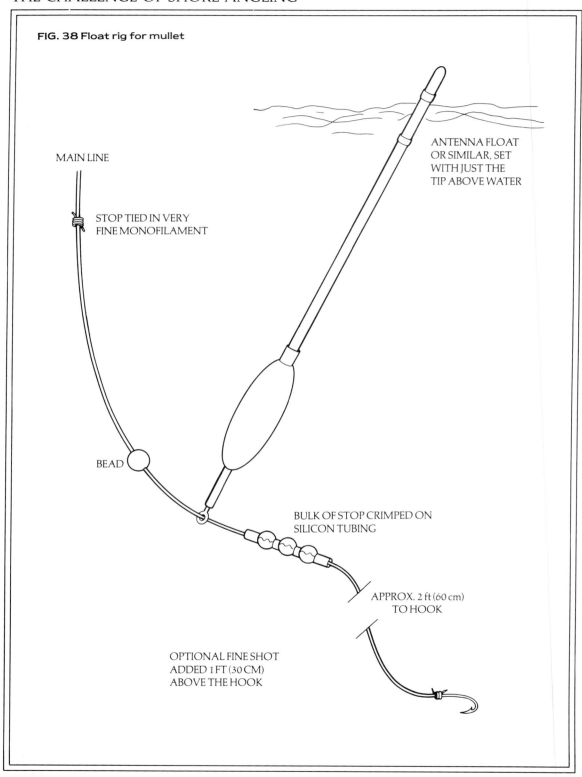

FIG. 38 Float rig for mullet

ANTENNA FLOAT
OR SIMILAR, SET
WITH JUST THE
TIP ABOVE WATER

MAIN LINE

STOP TIED IN VERY
FINE MONOFILAMENT

BEAD

BULK OF STOP CRIMPED ON
SILICON TUBING

APPROX. 2 ft (60 cm)
TO HOOK

OPTIONAL FINE SHOT
ADDED 1 FT (30 CM)
ABOVE THE HOOK

blanked, for him to be mobile, armed with a variety of baits and try his luck elsewhere. He might also have groundbaited, but the danger in this is that you might wean the shoal off your hookbaits and on to the finer particles in the groundbait. It is trial and error. But once you have established what baits are effective at what marks, combined with what tackle you used, the chances are that this combination will meet repeatedly with success. Remember that the bulk of the mullet diet is actually algae and diatoms, so no bait will be ideal.

TACKLE

For mullet, tackle must be both light and refined. It is no use expecting your beachcaster to double as a mullet rod when what you need is either a freshwater carp or match rod. I use a very cheap match model and find that it does the job very well, especially since I team it up with a reasonable quality, rear-drag fixed-spool filled with 4–6 lb (1.8–2.75 Kg) line.

Terminal tackle is illustrated in Fig. 38. I nearly always use float tackle, but an alternative is a running leger set-up in which the weight has been replaced with a freshwater swimfeeder. This second method is very useful when mullet are feeding on smaller foodstuffs, especially when they are responding to maggots, either coloured or scented. However, I get a kick out of float tackle, I love to see it slipping away, so I prefer to use it wherever possible. The float's shape does not matter greatly, as long as it does not carry much weight and is slim, so offering less resistance to a taking fish. Therefore I usually stick to antenna floats, which have an eye at the bottom. The float's body goes underwater, with very little above the surface, and what is above water is so light that it presents little or no resistance to the slightest knock.

You will notice that I group the (non-toxic) split shot and fasten them onto a piece of the very fine silicon tubing used with pole floats. The silicon is on the line to protect it when you crimp the shot together, but also to enable you to slide the shot to a different location without damaging the line. If you feel that you want some more shot near the bait, perhaps to sink it to what you think is the feeding zone, then do not place it any nearer to the hook

Tim Mather, aged 12, and a 3-lb mullet

than 1 ft (30 cm). Any closer and the bait will sink unnaturally fast, alerting the instincts of the fish.

For hooks I use freshwater models, ranging from size 8 down to size 18. I use these once and throw them away, as the salt water corrodes them too quickly for their lifespan to embrace more than one session. It is also fatal to put a hook back into a packet. Not only will it corrode, but it will take several others with it and dull the rest. Far better is one hook–one trip.

Other methods of fishing for mullet include spinning, which is particularly effective for thin-lips, free-lining, which is only possible from marks overlooking the water or from a moored boat, and fly fishing. The last is often the most erratic, sometimes scoring well and sometimes very badly. It is pretty hit and miss, although it can be good when it works.

Mike holds another good mullet

SPINNING

The most consistent scorer, certainly for thin-lips, is spinning. This is usually done with a blade spinner such as an ABU Droppen, the treble having been replaced with a size 8 hook on a 2 in (5 cm) trace. Tie the trace to the lure, but then whip the hook to the trace. If you have ever tried tying two knots only inches apart, you will know how much the line twists. Using a whipping for the hook prevents excessive twisting.

To spin the tackle, you first need to bait the hook with a tiny harbour ragworm. The blade attracts the mullet's attention, while the worm is the appetizer, depending on how fast you retrieve the tackle. The optimum speed would seem to be a medium retrieve, depending on how actively the fish are feeding. If they are hitting the lure quickly, being very near the surface, then sometimes a fast approach can work wonders. On the other hand, they might be skulking near the bottom, and then a slow retrieve is best.

If you tie a second swivel on the line, just before you attach the spinner, line twist will be lessened. This stops loops forming on the reel, which take precious time to remove.

When you catch a mullet, you will find that it is a fast-fighting fish, but that it can be controlled with judicious pressure from the rod tip. However, be careful with this as the mullet has a membrane behind the lip which can split very easily. Quite often the hook lodges in this membrane and the use of force will simply pull the hook from its mouth. It is better to have the drag on your reel loosened to allow the fish to run against pressure. Some anglers slacken the drag off almost completely, increasing resistance by braking the rim of the spool with the thumb.

Mullet will usually run, dive, run and swim towards you, all the while trying to dislodge the hook. This sequence varies from fish to fish, but they are usually pretty agile in the water. So stay alert on the strike in case they try some fancy acrobatics.

The bites can vary considerably: sometimes the float is pulled down very slowly while at other times it disappears in a flash. The strength of the take can be dramatic. Sometimes the float shoots

Mullet from a rocky mark

away underwater, or the spinner stops dead; at other times a gentle pluck is all the indication you will get.

Mullet like warm, settled weather, so June, July and August are usually the best months, although thick-lips can be found right through a mild winter in some areas. The mullets' preference for warmer waters may be a factor in their liking for estuaries, though salinity is probably the overriding motivation. Mullet move up and down the estuaries according to the movements of the tides and the amount of fresh (rain) water. Thick-lips seem to prefer greater salinity, and in an estuary containing both thick-lipped and thin-lipped mullet, the former wil be closest to the open sea.

Love them or hate them, fishing for mullet

demands your attention and patience more than almost any other branch of the sport. If you want to try it you must resolve not to be easily discouraged. There may be several sessions without bites, often made all the worse because you can see the fish swim right up to your bait and then apparently lose interest. Once in a while a tiny lift of the rod stimulates a take, the mullet perhaps being fooled into thinking that its meal is disappearing. But more often than not, it does not. Try to adopt a positive attitude. Some mullet seem more difficult to catch because they are just lazily cruising in the shallows, ignoring everything else with almost complete indifference. The chances are that these have already fed somewhere else. If you can find their feeding stations and gear both your tackle and approach to the situation, you will catch mullet. Just take time and persevere.

CHAPTER TWELVE

Cod and Whiting

Both of these species belong to the same family, as do the pollack, coalfish, pouting and ling. The pouting I am not going to discuss in any detail as it is not a question of how to catch them that concerns most anglers but how, once darkness has fallen, not to. Suffice it to say that all methods that work for whiting will also catch pouting. Ling belong firmly in the boat-fishing category, most often being taken over wrecks. Instead I shall concentrate on cod, which grow to over 5 ft (1.5 m) long and whiting, which peak at around 2 ft (60 cm), both of which species are essentialy winter targets for the majority of shore anglers.

HABITATS AND HABITS

Both species are caught from a variety of habitats, being found all around our coasts. However, the main distribution of cod is firmly in the North, and southern anglers encounter this species far less frequently from the shore than they do from boats. Sometimes cod are resident in rocky, weed-strewn areas, a situation demanding rotten-bottom or otherwise adapted tackles, at other times they prowl around beaches, piers, harbours or wherever there is a good supply of food. Fast tides are also a sign of good cod-holding grounds, but you may encounter problems with masses of floating weed.

Beachcasting tackle is usually a must when fishing for cod, particularly during daylight, when they roam a long way from the shore. Cod seem to lose their caution at night, prowling closer inshore and sometimes into quite shallow water, but at day you will generally need all the distance you can get, depending on where you fish. The determining factor is usually depth of water, a good depth being essential for close casting through the day.

The detail of your tackle depends again on where you fish. Rocky bottoms will usually need much heavier lines than for casting over sand, where a 15 lb (7 Kg) main line and a 50 lb (23 Kg) leader are often all you need. Another factor is the amount of loose weed floating in the water. Light line may break if weed is excessive, not being up to the task of dragging in enormous bundles of it. It is of course the usual question of getting to know the area you want to fish.

Diet

Cod are bottom feeders, living on a varied diet that more or less reflects the environment in which you catch them. Their most important foods are crustaceans, molluscs and worms, in that order, or so surveys of their stomach contents suggest. By far the majority of anglers fish for cod with lugworm, mounting several on a large hook. The next most important baits are peeler crabs, squid, especially whole calamari, razorfish and other shellfish including clams and cockles.

The bigger cod are decided predators, adding whiting, sandeels, sprats and pouting, to name but a few, to their diet. When the sprat shoals mass inshore, you may find that cod become pre-occupied with them, gorging themselves on the superabundance of food. Here the only real chance is to use sprats as bait, but there you have the problem of obtaining a fresh supply. You can try shop-bought offerings, but generally these have been dead for too long to adequately compete with the freshness of their living relations. Try to imagine the scene underwater: there are thousands of bright,

A brace of southern cod

glittering sprats in the water, while on the bottom is a single dead sprat, well past its prime, dulled and perhaps mutilated by the cast.

The only ally that you have in this situation is the fact that your bait is a soft option. It may not look much, compared to the shoal in the water, but it smells a little more and it will not try to swim away. To scoop it up is more energy-conserving than to chase its cousins.

METHODS

To fish for cod, you need to put your bait where the fish expect to find it. This demands either leger or paternoster tackle, both of which need to be as streamlined as possible, reducing air resistance and enabling you to maximize the distance available through your casting. Generally the paternoster has the advantage if you are expecting smaller fish. With two or three hooks all laying up a scent trail together, there is more to attract the fish than the single legered bait. An alternative with the paternoster is to use a self-spacing tackle. This is a two-hook rig where the bottom hook is fixed in position above the weight, while the top hook is tied to a sliding boom that is left free-running on the line. After the cast, the first hook is positioned near the weight, while the second has been forced up the line by both air and water resistance, often fishing the full length of your leader from the other hook.

This is a good tactic if you are fishing from a shingle beach. Here the shingle descends in banks and gullies, the food being swept along the beach and collecting in the gullies. The fish form the habit of swimming along the gullies, gathering up food as they go. With a conventional paternoster, where the top hook is fixed in position, you may, although unaware of it, be fishing your baits on the top bank, while the fish, more interested in what is in front of their noses, swim along either above or below your bait without noticing it. With the spacing rig you are increasing the chance of at least one of your baits being in the right position.

You can make up three-hook versions of this tackle, as I have on several occasions. Unfortunately the tackle is more bulky and the loss of distance outweighs the advantages of the rig, certainly as far as cod are concerned. It does not matter for flatfish

or other small bottom feeders, for which it is a good alternative tactic, but generally the two-hook rig is more effective for cod.

Twin paternoster

Fig. 39 shows the twin paternoster, which is easy to make up, easy to fish, and effective. You may, however, find it strange when you catch a fish on the top hook. The bite rattles away on the rod tip, but when you strike you feel very little, at least for a few seconds. Reeling in brings you again into contact with the fish and keeps you there. What has happened is that the boom, running free on the line, has given the fish a little leeway to run either towards or away from you. When the weight catches up with the boom, the fish pulling instinctively away from the danger, you suddenly feel the full weight of the fish.

Some anglers worry that this means that you will not be able to get a firm hook hold, but I have never found it so. I think that the lack of resistance encourages the fish to bite more confidently than they might have otherwise. In fact, I cannot remember ever having lost a fish after I saw the bite, at least not on this tackle.

Most of the cod that you get on this gear will be small, although a big one turns up every so often. However, a plump codling is a tasty meal, especially if it weighs 4 or 5 lb (1.8–2.25 Kg). Get a good session in with such fish and there are few anglers who bemoan their fate. A point to consider, however, is that the majority of cod don't reach sexual maturity until they attain a length of 24 in (60 cm). Some precocious males have been recorded as mature at 18½ in (47 cm), but females mature later. Therefore a limit of 24 in (60 cm) will put you on the safe side, even if by a small margin.

Legering

For anglers who want to aim purely at the bigger cod, the leger is just as efficient as the paternoster. For playing the fish it does allow the angler a direct pull during the retrieve, by contrast with booms or other arrangements, which take a great deal of sideways stress. A distance pattern of rig is also available, taking advantage of carp beads (to which you attach the weight, replacing the link supplied

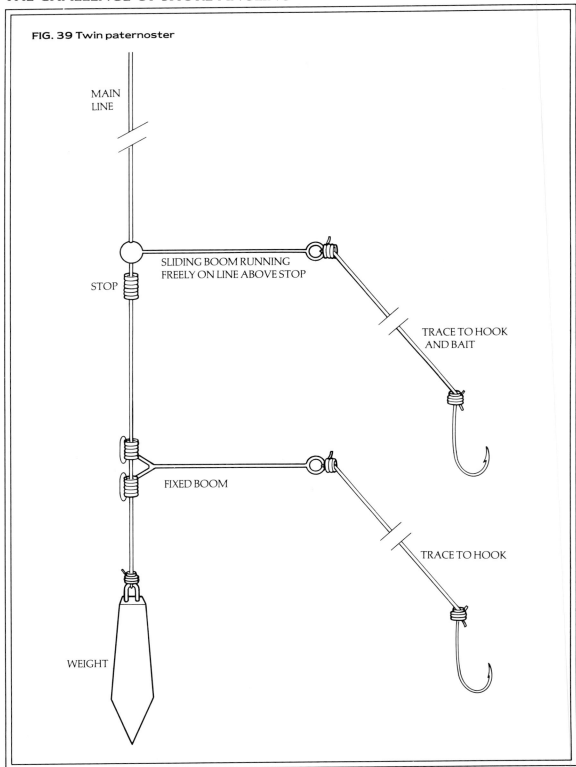

FIG. 39 Twin paternoster

MAIN LINE

STOP

SLIDING BOOM RUNNING FREELY ON LINE ABOVE STOP

TRACE TO HOOK AND BAIT

FIXED BOOM

TRACE TO HOOK

WEIGHT

Wilmek 'No-snag' weight

with a stouter oval link) and short lengths of plastic tubing (Fig. 40). Gravity keeps the trace and main line apart in the pre-cast. The extended bait clip keeps them apart during the cast.

Another option is the running leger plus tandem rig (Fig. 41). This is a trace with two hooks attached, the lower one being small and baited with worm, the upper being large and with the point presented clearly for easy penetration. In practise, the small bait attracts and hooks a small whiting, tethering it in the immediate vicinity of the larger hook. A cod or other predator attracted by the struggles of the smaller fish, comes along and eats it. As it does so, you get a chance to set the larger hook.

If your bait is continually shredded by smaller fish such as tiny whiting, then this is the time to experiment with a tandem rig. Quite often it produces an outsize fish, and not only cod, for it is also effective for other predators that may be in the

area. At different times of the year it will also take the occasional good bass.

Tackle-saving rig

The situations that I have dealt with so far all call for spiked leads, the presumption being that casting is over a clear bottom. However, there are locations where cod are taken in the middle of a kelp jungle, as they search for food among weed-ridden boulders and gullies. Here your approach must be different, the aim being not only to attract and hook the fish, but also to get your tackle out of harm's way as quickly as possible.

One method of doing this is to use a 'No-snag' flight made by Wilmek. This is a plastic vane that attaches the weight to the line but lifts the lead on the retrieve. The weight hangs down at one end and water resistance, acting against the vane, forces the tackle up through the water and fairly quickly to

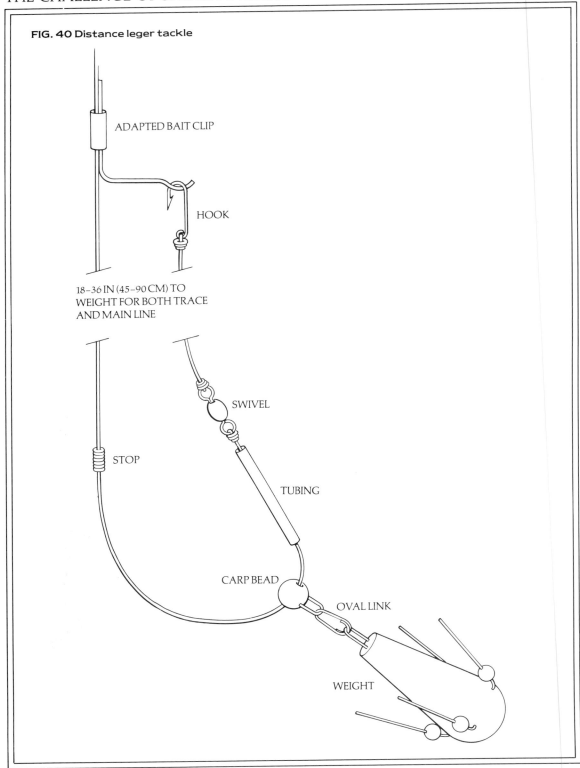

FIG. 40 Distance leger tackle

ADAPTED BAIT CLIP

HOOK

18–36 IN (45–90 CM) TO
WEIGHT FOR BOTH TRACE
AND MAIN LINE

SWIVEL

STOP

TUBING

CARP BEAD

OVAL LINK

WEIGHT

FIG. 41 Running leger plus tandem rig

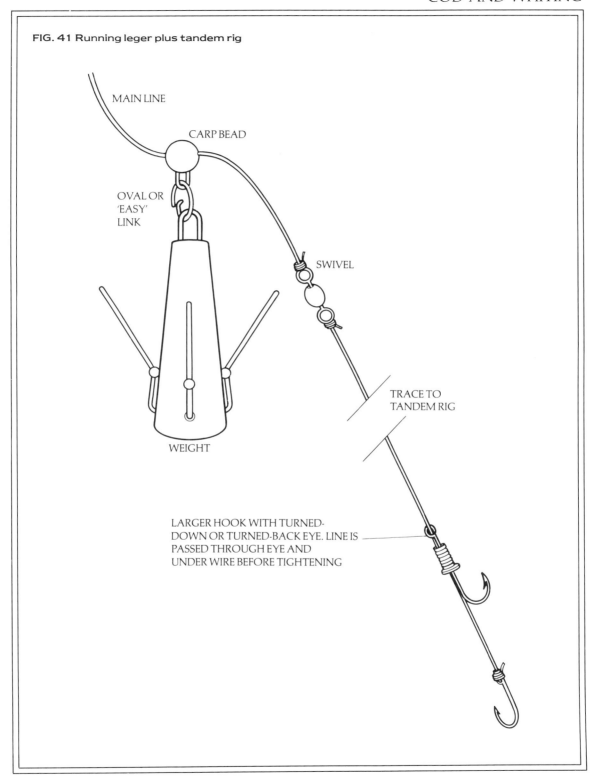

MAIN LINE

CARP BEAD

OVAL OR
'EASY'
LINK

SWIVEL

WEIGHT

TRACE TO
TANDEM RIG

LARGER HOOK WITH TURNED-
DOWN OR TURNED-BACK EYE. LINE IS
PASSED THROUGH EYE AND
UNDER WIRE BEFORE TIGHTENING

A whiting searches for food. Note the steamlined shape, built for the sudden rushes that give the angler the familiar rattle on the rod tip

the surface. For casting onto sand over rocks, such as headlands which give way to sand, Wilmek 'No-snag' weights are available, the vane being directly moulded into the weight itself. When I last bought some they were roughly the same price as a conventional Breakaway — excellent value for money. Wilmek weights are also available with quick-release wires.

Apart from using Wilmek weights or vanes, or the Breakaway plastic vane, which is based on the same principle, you can use conventional rotten-bottom tackle in much the same manner as for wrasse. Simply step up the size of both the hook and bait, bearing in mind that you are aiming at much bigger fish.

If you look at the photograph (p. 107), you will see the Wilmek quick-release model depicted. It is simple, neat and functional — an excellent idea and real value for money. I thoroughly recommend it.

If, despite all your precautions, you do get snagged up on the rocks there is often very little that you can do to get your tackle free. The first thing to try is to alter your angle of recovery. Give out slack line, walk a distance away, and then sweep the rod up while quickly recovering the line. Sometimes this will shift it, other times the slack will make the lead fall deeper into the crevice into which it has fallen, in which case you will have to pull for a break. Do this with the line wrapped around your clothing or a glove, not on your flesh as the line stretches under pressure and may cut into your skin like a cheesewire. Nor should you use the rod to try to pull your tackle free. It is a casting tool and a means of putting leverage on the fish — not a crane! Many rods are broken by this sort of abuse. Treat a rod well and it will reward you with many years of active service; treat it badly and it will probably let you down at the most inopportune moment.

Very often cod caught in weed-infested localities have a reddish tinge to their skin, earning them various nicknames in areas where this trait prevails. They may also give a vigorous fight, using the cover instinctively to their advantage. If you get a big one you will need to get it up and away from cover quickly, using the full length of your beachcaster to put leverage on it. At the same time you will have to judge the firmness of your hookhold as best you can from the strike. If you felt it connect firmly you can exert pressure accordingly.

Very often cod will give you a slack line bite, dragging the weight towards you instead of running in the opposite direction. By the time you have recovered the slack and struck into the fish, you may not have penetrated the flesh properly, securing a light hookhold that may be torn free by excessive force. You will have to play it by ear!

WHITING

Whiting are a much smaller species, and their combination of predatory traits and opportunism makes them easy to catch. The size of your hooks must be scaled down, but a three-hook paternoster is very often used by anglers wishing to build a good weight of fish very quickly. There is no problem about doing this, apart from the low individual weight of the fish.

If you want to target larger whiting stick to fish baits. It is not that worm baits will not catch them — they will, given the chance. It is just that worm baits are so attractive that smaller fish often shred them before the larger fish even see them. As a result you can get through bait very quickly, catch masses of fish and still have nothing decent to show for it at the end of the trip. But fish baits, by which I mean strips or whole sandeels, or similar baits, usually manage to connect with the bigger whiting sooner or later. Very often small whiting will mutilate fish baits as readily as they will worms, but a good-sized strip of mackerel can survive the attentions of the smaller fish longer than a worm, giving you more of a chance to connect with the big ones. It is all a question of tactics and what you find on the night,

although you may prefer catching smaller fish to taking nothing at all.

TACKLE

When the whiting are in you should not have any problem catching them, whether you use leger or paternoster. However, it is not very much fun reeling in two or even three fish that are completely outgunned. If you are beachcasting you do not have much choice, but there are some marks where you do, particularly from piers and harbour walls, even down the side of some headlands.

If distance casting is unnecessary you can scale your tackle down. On still nights, where the sea is calm and whiting run right up to the walls of the pier, try using a coarse-fishing rod with light float tackle and a Starlite attached. Set the depth to just off the bottom and experiment with your bait, sand shrimps and prawns being very effective on occasion, and mackerel strip also being very good.

When you catch a good whiting on this tackle, you will find that the fight you get is much better than normal, simply because the rod is much lighter than your beachcaster and so reacts well to the movements of the fish. Line strength is up to you, but I used to scale right down to breaking strains of about 1 lb (0.5 Kg). Nowadays I tend to stick to 4 lb (1.8 Kg) line, just in case I run into something a little bigger. If I do then I can, with judicious playing and lightly set drag, usually manage to get it to the net, in this case a pan landing net with a fibre-glass handle extendable to 7 ft (2 m).

This approach will undoubtedly give you more sport than simply reeling in a fish. If the sport does not matter to you and all you want is to catch fish, then stick with your beachcaster and follow the basic guidelines that either this book or other anglers will tell you. Whatever you decide, whether to experiment or not, I wish you success.

CHAPTER THIRTEEN

Hints for Disabled Anglers

A chance meeting led to the inclusion of this chapter, which deals with a subject of which at the time I had little experience. I was fishing off Brixham Breakwater, aiming to catch a few pollack, when I noticed a rather wistful expression on the face of the gentleman in the wheelchair behind me.

We started to chat and ended up making arrangements to go fishing.

While we chatted I lent Charles my spare rod, setting it up for float-fishing, with live prawns for bait. Almost straightaway he was into a pollack, taking five in the space of the hour for which we

Charles Armstrong on Paignton pier

The taper-trak in position . . .

talked. It was entertaining to both watch him fishing and listen to his conversation, but as I watched him very closely I began to turn over some ideas in my mind.

Since we first met, Charles and I have fished together several times, and I hope that we will continue to do so. On each occasion various problems have come to light, setting me thinking. The first of these was exactly where Charles could fish. Some beaches were fine, where the sand was firmly compacted and presented very little difficulty for the wheelchair, but there also had to be car parking very close to where we were going to fish. Other locations were piers and breakwaters, harbour walls and generally any flat concrete surface overlooking the sea. Bridges over estuaries, such as the bridge over the River Teign, were also possibilities as they stood a good chance of providing some entertaining sport with flounders in the autumn and towards Christmas.

At Brixham Breakwater, Charles and I usually end up fishing inside the harbour at the top of the tide, as close to the end as we can get. Since this is a considerable distance from the shore it enables us to cast into fairly deep water and catch a variety of species, principally, during the summer, wrasse, garfish, pollack, mackerel, scad, pouting, flatfish and eels. In the winter there should be coalfish and whiting, and the chance of a cod.

Setting up the rod, a task most of us take for granted, is not so simple when you are in a wheelchair. Sometimes you end up scraping the rod butt along the floor to reach the end rings, and there is a general inconvenience that increases with the length of the rod. To ease this process I suggested that Charles buy a telescopic rod, so that he could

. . . The taper-track in use

thread the line through the rings, tackle up and then extend the rod. Daiwa produces some good models for this purpose, but it will pay you not to go for the cheapest that you can find. Go for one that combines lightness and strength, for preference capable of casting either light float tackle or at least 2 oz (60 gm) of lead, and ideally being comfortable with 3 oz (85 gm). This will allow the use of either leger or float tackle.

Casting
(While the following section is primarily for disabled anglers, much of the advice is relevant for everyone.) Trying to cast from a wheelchair is inconvenient, to say the least. It tends to restrict the angler to an 'overhead thump'. With light tackle you can achieve a fair distance but you will not launch into a pendulum cast without considerable difficulty. I certainly would not attempt it, and indeed would regard it as impossible. Yet, overhead casting will still put you among fish. Charles, casting for himself, has caught mackerel, scad, garfish, pollack and wrasse since we started. There are also ways of casting a bit further if distance is important.

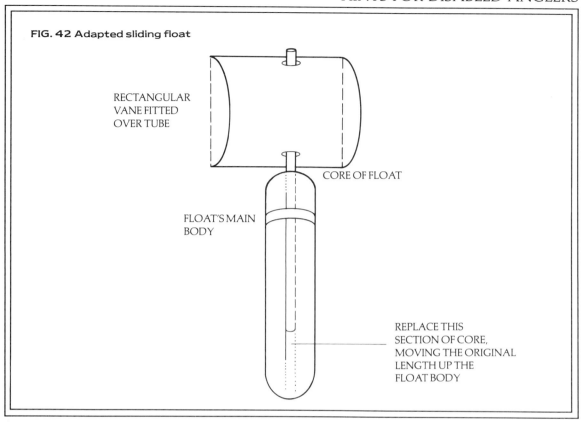

FIG. 42 Adapted sliding float

RECTANGULAR VANE FITTED OVER TUBE

CORE OF FLOAT

FLOAT'S MAIN BODY

REPLACE THIS SECTION OF CORE, MOVING THE ORIGINAL LENGTH UP THE FLOAT BODY

For legering, some anglers tie a partly inflated balloon to the line by a thin strand of cotton. The idea is to let the balloon drift the tackle a considerable distance from the shore, a gentle lob serving to start it off, then to strike hard with the rod. The cotton, weakened by the water, snaps, the balloon drifts off and the tackle sinks to the bottom. I tried this to see if it works, and it does, but you have to be careful when you use it. On some marks the balloon will head straight out to sea, on others it will drift at an angle or even parallel to the shore. On one occasion the balloon drifted out beautifully, running and running until I had nearly 300 yards (275 m) of line out. Then the *Pride of Paignton*, a pleasure cruiser, appeared around the headland and steamed straight over it, nearly pulling the rod from my hands before the line snapped.

If distance bothers you, then use the method. But it has the disadvantage that it can take a long time to get the tackle where you want it, wasting a lot of valuable fishing time. On balance, I think it is better to go for normal casting, especially as most of the available marks will have a sufficient depth of water to bring the fish close enough for you to reach by conventional methods.

I take a slightly different view for float-fishing, where I feel, at least for fishing during the low tide, that distance can change a blank couple of hours into at least a bite or two. In my teens, a long time before the freshwater piking equivalents appeared on the market, I experimented with vaned floats, prompted by the lift-bite indicator described on page 65.

Fig. 42 shows the vaned float that I use. Basically it is a West Country float that I have adapted. First I scrape the paint off the tubing that extends above and below the main body of the float. Then I insert a nail into the tubing at one end, to support the plastic, and clamp it into a vice. Judicious twisting of the float body exposes some 2½ in (6.5 cm) of

115

tubing. I then take a piece of plastic, cut from a plastic jar, lid or ice-cream container, make two holes in it, one at the top in the middle and one at the bottom, and put it on the tube. The vane has to bend over slightly to fit on the tubing, but grips sufficiently well to eliminate any worries that you might have over its security. For ease of visibility I like to use a coloured plastic rather than try to paint over something that does not take paint very well in the first place.

At the bottom of the float I insert a fresh piece of tube to ensure that the line continues to slide easily through the float. I then fish the float on sliding tackle as normal. The difference is that the vane acts as a sail, taking the float out further and faster than it would otherwise drift. However, unlike the leger tackle and the balloon method, the float tackle is fishing throughout its journey. More ground is covered and absolutely no fishing time is lost, unless the wind changes direction and starts blowing straight towards you.

This method does cover a lot of ground, but it will never win any awards for speed. It is a useful alternative tactic — even a deadly one — when used in the right place, at the right time. It also has the advantage that the vane increases the visibility of the float, being easily seen at far greater distances than the float on its own. Basically, check the wind is blowing in a useful direction and that the current is not so strong that the method will not work. If both factors are on your side you will be able to use the method with success.

In many places, the distance necessary to catch fish on float is far less than you might suspect. Take, for example, Paignton Pier. Charles and I visited it for an evening trip, fishing mackerel strip on float tackle at a depth of 7 ft (2 m). Charles stuck to fishing at fairly close range, certainly no more than 30 yards (27 m), while I aimed at the horizon. At the end of a couple of hours Charles had taken seven mackerel, two pollack, a scad and a garfish. I had two mackerel and three pollack.

Going for distance did not help on this occasion, but it serves to illustrate that the mark you fish will be the determining factor in whether you should hurl the tackle out or simply give it a gentle lob. On this occasion, the pier itself was the attraction, or rather the shoals of small baitfish that sought shelter in the ironwork underneath and all around. Casting a long way simply removed my bait from the principal feeding zone, whereas Charles was fishing in the midst of it.

Another problem was illustrated when we fished on Brixham Breakwater. Reeling tackle up the side was a hazardous process, rubbing the line and causing severe abrasion. When using float tackle this was most noticeable in the immediate vicinity of the weight, the hard metal edges of the drilled bullet biting into the line.

To counter this problem, which was aggravated by the weight being free-sliding, I introduced a telephone wire stop and a length of silicon tubing of extremely fine diameter (more often used for the wire stems of pole floats) into the tackle (Fig. 43). The stop went onto the main line, below the float, followed by a short length of silicon rubber, the weight, bead and the swivel, the latter tied to the end of the main line. The stop was tightened and pushed down the line as far as it would go, trapping the weight against the bead and swivel, but also trapping the silicon into position as an insert for the weight. Consequently abrasion of the line is much reduced and, as a bonus, there are fewer tangles.

One thing to watch for when float-fishing is that the hook may occasionally catch the line above the float. This means that the tackle tangles and, although the float may be sitting properly, the bait may be draped around it on the surface. The usual remedy is to check the line just before it hits the water. The float stops short, the bait flies ahead and the tackle hits cleanly and in good order.

While you are float-fishing, you will need to hold the rod for most of the time, ready to strike at the first sign of a bite. When you are legering, bites can sometimes be few and far between, and so the rod becomes a little tiring to hold and your interest starts to flag.

You can always put the rod in a rest, but to reach it quickly enough to strike a bite may cause a few problems. A telephone call to Dennis Perrin of MPH Associates proved very useful, Dennis being kind enough to send a sample of a device known as a taper-trak. This is a pole or rod rest that Dennis designed to fit on the side of a tackle box. It has

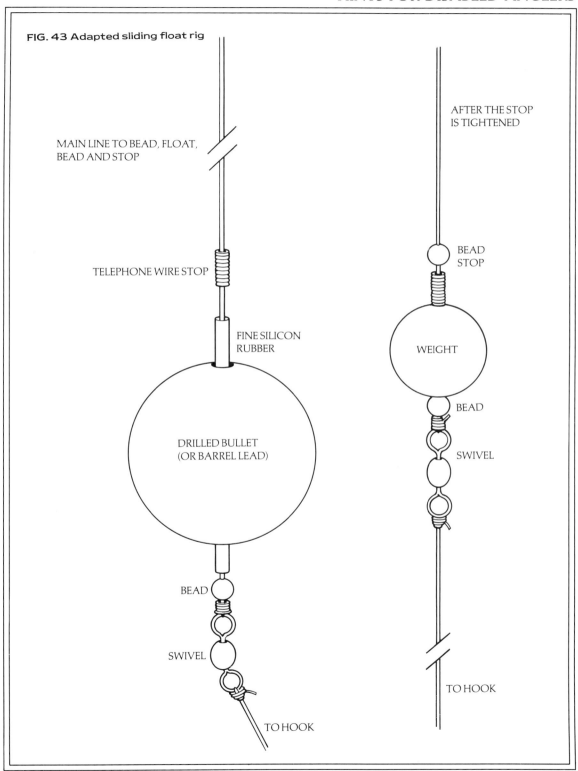

FIG. 43 Adapted sliding float rig

MAIN LINE TO BEAD, FLOAT, BEAD AND STOP

AFTER THE STOP IS TIGHTENED

TELEPHONE WIRE STOP

BEAD STOP

FINE SILICON RUBBER

WEIGHT

DRILLED BULLET (OR BARREL LEAD)

BEAD

SWIVEL

BEAD

SWIVEL

TO HOOK

TO HOOK

detachable arms, cushioned to prevent damage to the rod, and is both quick and easy to set up.

The trick was to secure the taper-trak to Charles's wheelchair. The chair belongs to the Department of Health, and so what was needed was a way of permanently attaching the device to the wheelchair without causing any damage, or any inconvenience to Charles. The solution was to first make a cardboard template of the chair arm. (The arms are removable and ideally positioned to take the taper-trak.) The template took into account the wheels and the brake on the right-hand side of the chair. We used it to cut a piece of plywood that could be fixed to the arm and to which, in turn, the taper-trak could be bolted.

To secure the wood to the arm, we traced the position of the metal struts onto the back of the wood. We then drilled the wood, not the chair, in several places to both sides of the metal. Wire was passed around both the metal and the wood, one piece to each pair of holes, then twisted tightly to hold the wood in position. It was important that some wire went between the top of the frame and the wood, to ensure that the wood did not slip downwards and interfere with either the brake or the wheels. If you look at the photograph you will see that we cut two arches out of the wood to accommodate both of these features.

To show how secure the taper-trak is, the photograph demonstrates it holding a 12 ft (3.5 m) beachcaster. As this is a much heavier rod than a telescopic, you can be confident about both the fitting and the taper-trak itself. Take a little time and care to do the job properly and it should not let you down. If for any reason you have to return the chair, all you need do is to snip the wire with a pair of pliers. The wood will come free and the chair will be completely undamaged. Another point, both for the sake of appearance and protection of the wood, is to give it a coat of paint, preferably black to blend in with the chair. The last thing of all is to bend the ends of the twisted wire, which we put on the inside of the frame, flush to the wood and coat them with a blob of Araldite to prevent them catching on your clothes.

The taper-trak is not expensive — about £10 at the time of writing — but it is a valuable aid for the disabled angler. It is convenient and, fitted as described above, ideally positioned for quick and easy striking. When Charles legers, he rests his hand on the rod. A strike straight upwards, swivelling the butt downwards at the same time that the rod tip is lifted, both sets the hook and removes the rod from the rest.

I should also mention the choice of line. When fishing from piers and breakwaters you often have to winch the fish up a vertical drop or drag it over the side. In either case it is best to increase the strength of the line to give you some reserve strength. I would not recommend a breaking strain at less then 12 lb (5.5 Kg), and 20 lb (9 Kg) would be safer. If you want to fish lighter, fine: there are many marks where you can do just that. However, I would strongly recommend that you obtain a spare spool for your reel, keeping one spool for heavier line and the other for lighter.

I have not mentioned beaches in much detail, as sand is a little awkward for some chairs. But watch out for places where roads run parallel to the beach, or indeed any mark where you can reach the water both safely and with little inconvenience. If you take yourself down onto the sand be sure that you know the exact position of the tides and give yourself plenty of time to be able to get back safely ahead of the incoming water.

Look inside harbours, for with parking often very close at hand, these can be convenient and give you access to some excellent fishing, especially in the early hours and at night. Shoals of coalfish and/or pollack may be resident, while mullet will usually appear during the summer. Whiting enter at night, and the bottom is often a fertile ground for flatfish. Unfortunately, they are even more fertile grounds for crabs, so fit a buoyancy device to lift your bait just slightly off the bottom.

Whatever fishing you decide to do, or wherever you go, don't be put off by practical difficulties or the attitudes of others. Sea fishing is great fun and as interesting as you want to make it. There are also a variety of related activities, such as bird-watching, fish identification, angling videos to watch, and evenings out with the local angling clubs. If you find it dull or boring, you are probably doing something wrong.

Index

Page references in *italics* refer to diagrams and photographs.